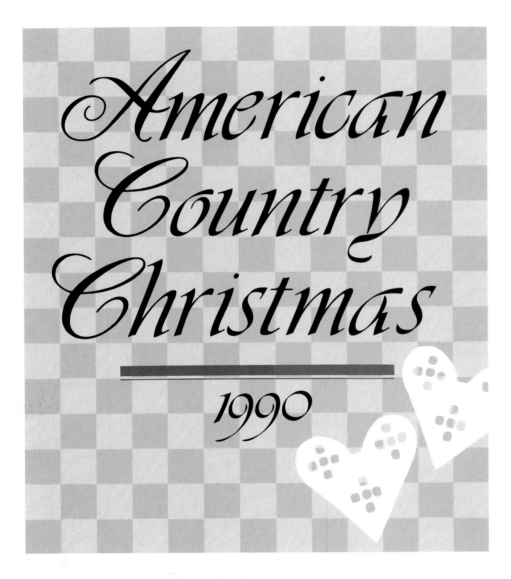

American Country Christmas

1990

COMPILED & EDITED BY
PATRICIA DREAME WILSON

Oxmoor House®

©1990 by Oxmoor House, Inc.
Book Division of Southern Progress Corporation
P.O. Box 2463, Birmingham, Alabama 35201

Library of Congress Catalog Number: 89-61909
ISBN: 0-8487-1027-4
ISSN: 1044-4904
Manufactured in the United States of America
First Printing

Executive Editor: Nancy J. Fitzpatrick
Production Manager: Jerry Higdon
Associate Production Manager: Rick Litton
Art Director: Bob Nance
Copy Chief: Mary Jean Haddin

American Country Christmas 1990

Editor: Patricia Dreame Wilson
Assistant Editor: Karen Broun Brookshaw
Contributing Editors: Charlotte Hagood,
   Cecilia C. Robinson
Senior Designer: Cynthia R. Cooper
Editorial Assistant: Lelia Gray Neil
Production Assistant: Theresa L. Beste
Assistant Copy Editor: Susan Smith Cheatham
Artists: Barbara Ball, Karen L. Tindall

Recipe Development: Elizabeth Taliaferro
Test Kitchen Home Economist: Kathleen Royal

To find out how you can order *Cooking Light* maga-
zine, write to *Cooking Light*®, P.O. Box C-549,
Birmingham, AL 35283.

Contents

Introduction 1

Country Christmas at Home

An Old-Fashioned Farmhouse Christmas 4
Elegant Swags for Your Mantel 10
Log Cabin Holidays 12
Welcome the Season 14
The Warmth of Crafts 16
Keepsake Collection 18
Weave a Courtier's Knot with Wheat 19
Ideas: The Magic of Candlelight 22

Holiday Handiwork

Angels and Stars Herald the Season 26
Believe in the Magic of Christmas 28
Mary Engelbreit's Painted Pillows 32
A Christmas Cardigan 34
Dancing Through the Holidays 36
A Colonial Christmas in Cross-Stitch 39
Letter-Perfect Cross-Stitchery 42
Santa Steps Out in Checks and Plaids 44
Prairie Garlands 47
Adapt a Coverlet Design 48
Little Miss Peep and Her Sheep 50
Greetings for the Holidays 54
Ideas: Try Stamping: It's Worth Repeating . . . 56

Treasured Traditions

A Patriotic Christmas 60
Colonial Drum and Fife Inspiration 67
Early Settlers' Christmas 68
Victorian Paper Ornaments 70
The Sweet Life 73
Quillwork: Filigree Made from Paper 76
Ideas: The Fragrance of Christmas 78

A Country Christmas Pantry

The Perfect Gift: Chocolate 82
Bake a Batch of Citrus Treats 88
Share the Sweetness 94
Canning Jar Recipe Holder 96
O Christmas Cheese! 97
Fruit Basket Ornaments 102
Homespun Desserts 103
Ideas: Easygoing Entertaining 110

Pleasures of the Season

Host a Holiday Tea 114
The Christmas Tree 120
Carolers Sing for Their Supper 122
Ideas: Surprising Packages 126

Patterns 128
Contributors 154
Index 155

*Y*ear after year, memories are made at Christmas. We plan far in advance—sometimes starting December 26—to create a special season for our loved ones. We work hard to make a holiday for our children as homey and unforgettable as the ones from our childhoods.

Our plans begin with the gift list: *What will I give Grandmother this year? Would my baby sister like a hand-knit cardigan? What about Bo Peep and her sheep for my little niece?*

Months are spent choosing fabrics and yarns in colors just right, sewing ornaments and dolls, and, along in November, preparing tins filled with treats. After the gifts are lovingly finished, the wrapping, decorating, and baking begin.

We bring down the boxes from the attic and sort through years of handmade decorations to uncover more memories. *Remember when Daddy cut out these tin stars for the tree? Where's the old Santa we made from red wool for the treetop?*

So the tree becomes glorious. The packages begin to pile up. Dad hangs a garland over the door. Another batch of cookies bakes in the oven. Carols are playing on the stereo. At last, Christmas Day arrives. All the planning, sewing, baking—all the love and care add up to another holiday filled with sweet memories.

We at Oxmoor House prepare *American Country Christmas* for you in much the same way. We spend months planning, designing, photostyling, photographing, and traveling to bring these holiday ideas together. Then comes the gift wrapping—the writing, editing, proofreading, and rewriting. The year seems very short sometimes. Before we know it, we must send the book off to you. We hope the projects, stories, ideas, and recipes here will help you to make happy memories for your family this Christmas.

We offer you our year of work with love . . . and a wish for a merry, country Christmas.

Patricia D. Wilson

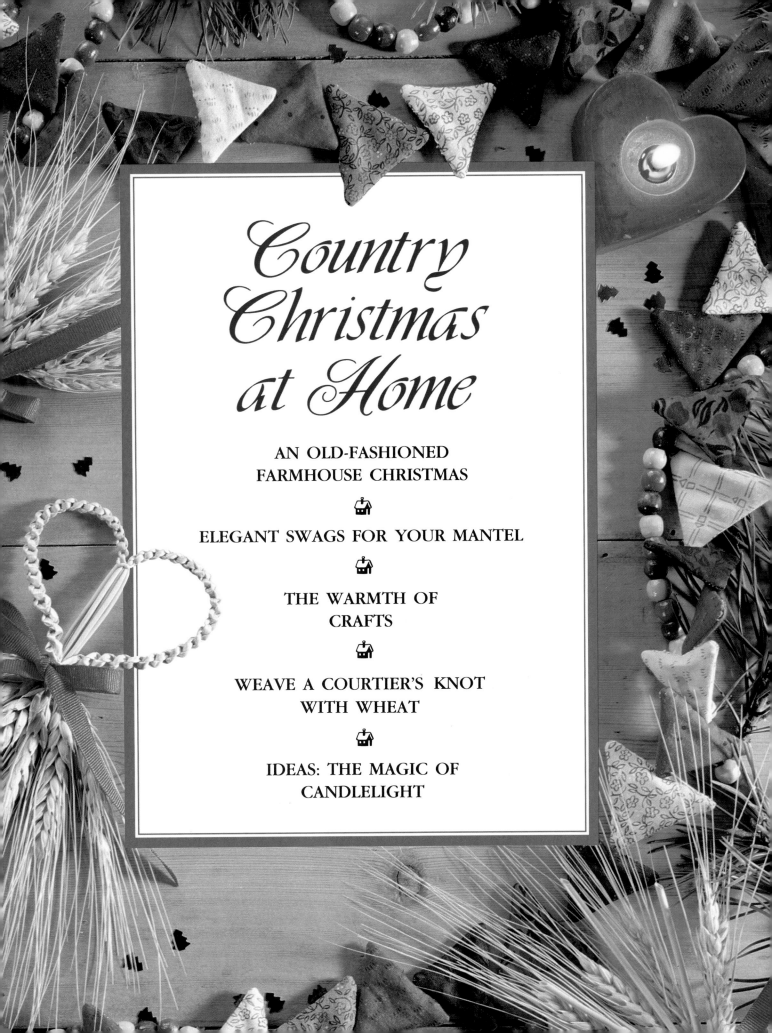

Country Christmas at Home

AN OLD-FASHIONED
FARMHOUSE CHRISTMAS

ELEGANT SWAGS FOR YOUR MANTEL

THE WARMTH OF
CRAFTS

WEAVE A COURTIER'S KNOT
WITH WHEAT

IDEAS: THE MAGIC OF
CANDLELIGHT

An Old-Fashioned Farmhouse Christmas

"I have no master plan. I decorate for the holidays in a haphazard way," Barbara Hood says.

When you look around her West Grove, Pennsylvania, farmhouse, Barbara's words are hard to believe. In every corner a cheerful scene greets the eye. The rooms are warmly decorated with teddy bears, antique toys, and Santas. Every window frames a fresh green wreath. But as Barbara swirls around the house, rearranging here and there, you can see that her decorating is certainly spontaneous. She just seems to have a knack for putting things in exactly the right places.

Above: A wreath graces every window of the Hoods' fieldstone farmhouse. The sleigh, found in Lancaster County, Pennsylvania, was Barbara's Christmas gift from Dick one year. During Christmas open house, Santa greets guests from the sleigh.

Left: Traditionally, Barbara, Dick, their daughters, and Barbara's parents all share a Christmas Eve dinner of steak and oysters in this dining area. Everyone opens one special present after dinner. If curiosity gets the best of them, they also check their stockings.

On the mantel, miniature dried pineapples punctuate a garland of apple slices strung on blue-check homespun. Mountain laurel roping contrasts nicely with the red of the apple and the colonial red of the mantel.

5

It helps, of course, to have such a fine place to decorate. Barbara and her husband, Dick, have restored their fieldstone house to its picture-perfect 18th-century state. In the 259 years since the house was built, only three families have called it home. William Penn, the founder of Pennsylvania, deeded the property to his daughter Letitia. Her house was built in 1731. Robert Strawbridge, a Philadelphia lawyer, was the next owner. In 1930 Dick's father, Charles, bought the farmstead. Dick and Barbara purchased it from Charles in 1962.

With so much history to bring to life, Barbara and Dick have tackled the farmhouse's continual restoration with energy. Their combination of inventive decoration and enthusiastic renovation adds up to a home full of old-fashioned Christmas spirit.

"Everything I use to decorate I find lying around my house. I just use it in different ways at Christmas," Barbara says. She describes one such "discovery"—a mantel decoration—this way: "I like to collect teddy bears and toys. So at Christmas I gathered all I had together in a wagon and pulled them around the house until we came to the living room. They looked so

Opposite: This intimate living room offers abundant country charm. Artist Gail Griffith created the Santa in his sleigh. The antique straw-stuffed horse in the window is covered in black wool. It stands on a stenciled wooden platform with iron wheels.

Above: The kitchen holds one of the house's three Swedish-style corner fireplaces. The red cabinets on top are actually warming cupboards, once used to keep baked goods warm. Barbara brightens her navy, red, and white kitchen with bunches of dried golden yarrow and a splash of red chili peppers.

Left: This band is ready to strike up some jolly Christmas carols.

7

happy when I set them up on the mantel. I decided they ought to have music and added the toy instruments."

For Barbara and Dick, Christmas really begins in October when they decorate Barbara's antique shop, just across the yard from the house, for an open house celebration. Her shop breathes with the atmosphere of an old-time general store. Dick makes garlands and wreaths from evergreens growing on the property. Barbara decorates five Christmas trees for the shop. Then after Thanksgiving Day she dresses up nine more inside the farmhouse.

When Barbara talks about Christmas, the energy bubbles to the surface in a great rush. "When I was a child, my parents made the holiday so special for me that I just didn't ever want it to end," Barbara says. "For two months Dick and I live and breathe Christmas. In January, when everybody else takes down their lights, we're sad to say, 'Guess we have to stop now.' "

Even after the lights come down and the wreaths are tossed away, Barbara leaves a secret clutch of Santas in her shop year-round for Christmas enthusiasts like herself.

Opposite: Morning sunlight dapples the stone smokehouse built in 1795. Barbara's Country Store was built onto the side of this building.

Above: Buffy, the family dog, and one of many barn cats wait for their chance at a sip of morning milk brought up from the barn.

Below: Dick makes all the wreaths, including the Williamsburg-style apple fan above the door.

Elegant Swags for Your Mantel

These smart mantel swags can add dramatic style to your holidays. The green moiré swag is accented with bows that match its bright red lining. The plaid swag trimmed with large ruffled buttons offers a bright country look. And for gift wrap that coordinates with your mantel decoration, the covered buttons are quick to make.

Swags, which require very little cutting and stitching, are also an effective decorating touch for an archway or doorway.

Red and Green Taffeta Swag

Materials for 1 swag and 4 bows:
6½ yards (45″-wide) red taffeta
5 yards (45″-wide) green moiré taffeta
matching thread
pushpins

Note: Dimensions given are for a 75″ mantel. Adjust dimensions according to length of mantel.

To make swag, cut 1 (25″ x 148″) piece each from red taffeta and from green taffeta. To make diagonal corner, measure 22½″ from bottom corner on 1 end down long side of red fabric. Mark. Draw a line from this mark to top corner of same end. Cut along line. Repeat on other end and on both ends of green fabric.

With right sides facing and raw edges aligned, stitch red and green fabric together with ½″ seam, leaving 6″ opening on 1 long side for turning. Turn and press. Slipstitch opening closed.

To make ribbons for bows, cut 4 (8″ x 63″) strips from red taffeta. With right sides facing and raw edges aligned, fold 1 strip in half lengthwise. To make diagonal corner, measure 3½″ from bottom corner on 1 end down long side. Mark and cut as for swag. Stitch raw edges with ½″ seam, leaving opening for turning. Finish as for swag. Repeat to make 3 more ribbons.

To drape swag, measure an equal amount of fabric to hang from each end of mantel. Gather fabric at these points and wrap tightly with

thread. Knot thread to secure. Measuring an equal distance in from first ties, repeat. (See photograph.) Tie bows. Stitch 1 bow to swag at each thread-wrapped section. Attach swag to mantel with pushpins.

Plaid Taffeta Swag

Materials for 1 swag and 4 buttons:
5 yards (50″-wide) red-and-green plaid taffeta
¾ yard (45″-wide) red taffeta
¾ yard (45″-wide) green taffeta
matching thread
4 (3″) buttons (to cover)
hot-glue gun and glue sticks
pushpins

Note: Dimensions given are for a 75″ mantel. Adjust dimensions according to length of mantel.

To make swag, with right sides facing and raw edges aligned, fold plaid fabric in half lengthwise. To make diagonal corners, measure 26″ from bottom corner on each end down long side. To cut and stitch, repeat procedure for ribbons for Red and Green Taffeta Swag.

To drape swag, repeat procedure for Red and Green Taffeta Swag.

To cover buttons, cut 4 (4″) squares from scraps of plaid fabric. Following manufacturer's instructions, cover buttons.

For ruffles around buttons, cut 4 (4″ x 22″) bias strips from green fabric and 4 (3″ x 21″) bias strips from red fabric. With wrong sides facing and raw edges aligned, fold 1 strip in half lengthwise. With ¼″ seam, stitch ends of strip together. Run 2 rows of gathering stitches close to raw edges and pull to gather ruffle to fit around button. Repeat for all strips. Placing 1 red ruffle on top of 1 green ruffle, stitch together along gathering threads. Using hot-glue gun, glue 1 covered button on top of red and green gathered ruffles. Repeat for 3 remaining buttons.

Stitching through shank on back of buttons, tack buttons to swag at each thread-wrapped section. Attach swag to mantel with pushpins.

Left: A plaid-covered, ruffle-trimmed button makes a colorful package topper. Use scraps of plaid fabric for the ribbon.

Right: A single lantern light glows against the snowy afternoon sky. In the background stands the Lincoln Log House—two simple rooms connected by a dogtrot.

Log Cabin Holidays

On New Year's Eve of 1976, John and Jane Frank of St. Charles, Missouri, welcomed party guests to celebrate the completion of a log cabin—the second one built on their property to honor Abraham Lincoln. They offered their guests bread baked fresh in a fireplace oven, just as young Abe might have enjoyed it. They felt a deep satisfaction during this celebration, for the cabin, which they named the Lincoln Log House, had just been moved to St. Charles. The cabin had been built in 1840 in Troy, Missouri, by the family of explorer Meriwether Lewis.

The Franks placed the Lincoln Log House, the second cabin endeavor, about 50 yards behind their own home, which was the first. Over the years, they had added on to their log cabin home by using logs from five different structures. And in 1984 they built another log building, a chapel, just beyond the Lincoln Log House.

The Franks' admiration of Lincoln and his rise from his boyhood log cabin to the White House became a focal point in their lives. They were passionate about sharing their love for the Great Emancipator. John and Jane would welcome visitors to their home, eager to teach them about Lincoln and what his childhood might have been like growing up in a one-room log cabin. John also gained an artistic reputation for his likenesses of Lincoln, done in watercolor, wood, and bronze.

John passed away two years ago. Now Jane continues to spread their love of Lincoln and the pioneer way of life. School children regularly tour Jane's home, the Lincoln Log House, and the chapel, guided by history lessons from Jane, a retired first-grade teacher.

When she's not giving tours, Jane runs an antique business in her home and travels around the country, making purchases for a few special clients. And at Christmas she continues the family tradition of cutting a cedar big enough to touch the beamed ceiling in the living room of her log cabin home. Christmas there echoes with a traditional American character that would have put Mr. Lincoln right at ease.

Above: At Christmastime Jane places quaint playthings from her antique shop around the cedar tree and on the mantel. The horse rocker, known as a shoofly, was made at the turn of the century. Jane holds Precious, a furry toy monkey who comes alive in her hands, moving his head and arms.

Below: The back porch creaks under a happy load of wooden collectibles. A butcher block shows off the layered colors of paint it has collected in its 125 years. A dark blue floral pattern accents the warm red paint of the sled.

Above: This dappled gray rocking horse, with a real horsehair mane and tail, was carved by John as Jane's Christmas gift in 1976. A year earlier he had carved one for their grandson. The hand-colored Lincoln notecard was sketched by John.

Left: The Franks built this chapel from 100-year-old logs left over from the construction of their log cabin home, combined with logs from friends.

Even though it has no heat or electricity, the chapel serves as a site for weddings. One was held just before Christmas last December. The bride draped quilts over the pews to bundle the guests when the chill took hold.

Welcome the Season

Welcome the holiday season with this sewing project that combines cross-stitch, appliqué, and quilting. The complementary fabric and floss colors carry the theme from one technique to another. The top center panel of cross-stitched sheep and flowers is echoed in the surrounding appliquéd pieces. A sawtooth border and outline quilting accent this handsome piece.

Below: This wall hanging is a sampler of techniques. Tiny jingle bells on the appliquéd sheep create a three-dimensional effect.

Welcome Wall Hanging

Materials:
completed cross-stitch (for chart and color key with instructions, see page 148)
pattern on page 150
placement diagram on page 151
1 yard (45″-wide) off-white fabric
½ yard (45″-wide) dark green miniprint
⅓ yard (45″-wide) red miniprint
scraps of solid dark red for center flower
¼ yard (45″-wide) tan pindot
24″ (⅛″-wide) black ribbon
4 small jingle bells
plastic template material
water-soluble fabric marker
39″ x 33″ piece of batting
39″ x 33″ piece of fabric for backing

Note: 100% cotton fabric is recommended. All seam allowances are ¼″.

Trim cross-stitched piece to 6" x 10½".

From off-white fabric, cut 2 (6" x 6½") pieces (B). (Refer to placement diagram for references to quilt pieces.) From green miniprint, cut 2 (1" x 6½") strips (1A). With right sides facing, sew 1 edge of strip 1A to 1 (6") edge of cross-stitch piece (A). Repeat for opposite edge of A. Trim seams. With right sides facing, sew 1 (6") edge of piece B to strip 1A. Repeat to join remaining piece B to opposite edge of pieced unit.

From green miniprint, cut 1 (1" x 23") strip (2A). With right sides facing, sew 1 edge of strip 2A to bottom edge of pieced unit. From off-white fabric, cut 1 (11" x 23") rectangle (C). With right sides facing, sew rectangle to bottom of pieced unit.

Using paper-patch appliqué method (see instructions below), transfer appliqué pattern for flower and small leaf pieces to fabrics indicated and cut out. Follow placement diagram to appliqué flowers and leaves to center of squares B.

Following paper-patch appliqué method, transfer appliqué patterns for sheep, heart, rosebud, and large leaf pieces to fabrics indicated and cut out. Follow placement diagram to appliqué pieces to rectangle C.

To attach bells to sheep, cut ribbon into 4 (6") lengths. Tie 1 bell to center of 1 piece of ribbon. Make a small bow at top of bell. Referring to pattern, tuck 1 ribbon end under each appliquéd ear and tack to secure. Repeat for remaining sheep.

To form borders, from green miniprint, cut 2 (1¼" x 25") strips and 2 (1¼" x 19") strips (D). From off-white fabric, cut 2 (2½" x 29") strips and 2 (2½" x 23") strips (E). With right sides facing, center and sew 1 long edge of 1 strip D to a raw edge of pieced unit. Repeat step for remaining edges of pieced unit, mitering corners. Trim seams. With right sides facing, center and sew edges of strips E to raw edges of strips D, mitering corners. Trim seams.

Transfer triangle pattern (F) to template material and cut out. Cut 104 triangle pieces from each fabric indicated.

For the sawtooth border design, sew 1 green triangle to 1 off-white triangle with right sides facing. Referring to the placement diagram for the direction of the triangle pieces, continue sewing triangles together for top and bottom border of quilt (56 triangles each), for side borders (44 triangles each), and for corners (2

triangles each). With right sides facing, sew 1 sawtooth border strip to each raw edge of the pieced unit.

From red miniprint, cut 2 (1" x 32") strips and 2 (1" x 26") strips (G). With right sides facing, center and sew 1 edge of 1 strip G to 1 raw edge of pieced unit. Repeat for remaining edges of pieced unit, mitering corners. Trim seams.

From green miniprint, cut 2 (3" x 41") and 2 (3" x 31") strips (H). Attach strips H to pieced unit as for strips G above.

To quilt off-white border, using water-soluble marker, transfer heart and line quilting design onto border piece E as follows: 10 hearts along top and bottom borders and 7 hearts along side borders. (Refer to placement diagram.) Do not quilt yet.

Stack backing (right side down), batting, and top (right side up). Baste layers together, beginning at center and working toward edges.

Starting with appliqué pieces, outline-quilt ⅛" outside each piece. Quilt heart and line pattern on border E and quilt-in-the-ditch along all border seams. Remove basting. Slipstitch edges.

Paper-Patch Appliqué

Try using freezer paper when appliquéing small pieces. It acts as a guide for turning seam allowances. Here are 2 techniques:

Cut the finished-size appliqué shape from freezer paper and iron it, with shiny side *down,* onto the wrong side of the fabric. Cut the shape from the fabric, adding ¼" seam allowance all around edge. Clip curves and corners. Appliqué shape to the fabric, turning under seam allowance with the needle as you go. To remove paper after appliqué is complete, slash fabric beneath appliqué shape.

Or, cut finished-size appliqué shape from freezer paper. Place the paper shape, with shiny side *up,* on the wrong side of the fabric. Cut out and clip curves as above. Fold seam allowance over onto paper shape and iron in place. Iron appliqué shape onto the fabric. Appliqué in place; then remove paper as above.

The Warmth of Crafts

Gerry Kimmel, a quilt designer and shop owner, surrounds herself with various crafts. Handwoven coverlets, hand-hooked rugs, and hand-stitched quilts warm every room of her Liberty, Missouri, home.

The handmade collectibles add a touch of uncluttered fun. A single Santa dances on a plain grapevine wreath. A simple swag of princess pine sits atop a painting of a rural farm scene.

"It's so much fun to have handmade things," says Gerry.

She and her husband, Ron, both love clean

Below: Warmed by fire, sunlight, and wood tones, this living room/dining room combination highlights hand-carpentry and handcrafts.

simplicity and fine craftsmanship. This combination is evident in their home, a two-story Victorian converted into a casual country abode. Their "great" room was originally two separate rooms. The Kimmels took out a dividing wall, removed old floral wallpaper, and added a wood-beamed ceiling. They also uncovered fine hardwood floors, made from five kinds of lumber laid at odd angles.

After renovation, Gerry knew she didn't want the somber Victorian drapes that came with the house, so she asked Ron to build shutters. With Gerry's favorite star motif in mind, he carved out special five-pointed openings at the top of each shutter. Hoops of bittersweet, a year-round accent, were added to break up the large white squares of window.

At Christmastime, holiday crafts made by local artists deck the mantel and even the floor. Missouri artist Rosalee Zahnd and Nebraska artist Sandy Gerweck, for instance, made several of the Santas that grace the Kimmel home. A hand-hooked rug, alive with playful snowmen, lies by the hearth. Gerry asked her rug-hooking teacher, Emma Lou Lais, to suggest a pattern for a snowman rug; Emma designed the triptych of melting snowmen.

For Gerry, Christmas is a wonderful chance to warm the winter with glowing crafts.

Below right: A hand-carved Santa drives his goat sled across a blanket chest made by Ron's grandfather.

Left: The cross-stitched samplers transform an entranceway into a showcase of stitchery. These were stitched by Gerry's daughter, sister, and a few friends.

One of Gerry's quilt designs, Stars and Squares, is draped beside the feather tree.

Long, narrow frames become a holiday asset when used to frame antique or other special Christmas cards, as above. A grouped collection, top right, makes an even bigger splash when a length of red ribbon is used behind the frames to complement the mat board color.

Keepsake Collection

If you've ever been lured by the charm of antique postcards and Christmas cards, you know how irresistible they are and how they multiply. But over the years where does one put all these cards, these pretty pictures?

Amy Alfeld, of Alton, Illinois, knows the dilemma. "I went nuts for holiday postcards," she admits. Most of her own extensive collection was printed in Germany before World War I, an event that ended imports of lithographed German cards.

"Most people just keep their collection in a shoe box or something, but my husband and I had more than 300 cards. One day I spread them out on the dining room table. I found that several of them could be grouped together."

Amy positioned cards related to one another in theme or color on red mat board. She attached the cards to the mat with acid-free tape so that she could remove them later, if needed, without damage.

Her idea for framing them in long groupings led her to a new discovery—she could attractively decorate the narrow section between door frames with them. Today, her collection graces these and other small spaces in need of holiday touches.

Whether you use them to frame your doorway or as a brightener in a hallway, your own collection of Christmas cards—like Amy's—can add warm holiday memories to your home.

Weave a Courtier's Knot with Wheat

There was an old English custom that, when a lad came courting, he should be given a bundle of wheat to weave while visiting his sweetheart. When the weaving was done, his visit was at an end. Of course, the young man tried to keep weaving as long as possible in order to have a longer visit! If the courtship was successful, the woven wheat was placed on the wedding altar and then saved to use as an ornament on the couple's Christmas tree.

Courtier's Knot Wreath

Materials for 1 wreath:
60-70 (16″- to 18″-long) stalks of wheat
large terry-cloth towel
wallpaper tray or container to soak wheat
heavy-duty cotton thread

Note: See Diagram 1 for parts of stalk.

To make a straight stem for weaving, break off the bottom portion of 1 stem at the joint 2″ above the bottom. Remove leaves. Repeat for the remaining stems.

Wrap wheat in towel and place in wallpaper tray; soak in water for approximately ½ hour. (Length of soaking time varies with thickness of

Left: Here, four Courtier's Knots are tied together to make a Courtier's Knot Wreath. The wreath, along with two single knots at the top and bottom, is sewn to a 78-inch (2¼-inch-wide) grosgrain ribbon, doubled for strength, for a Christmas bellpull.

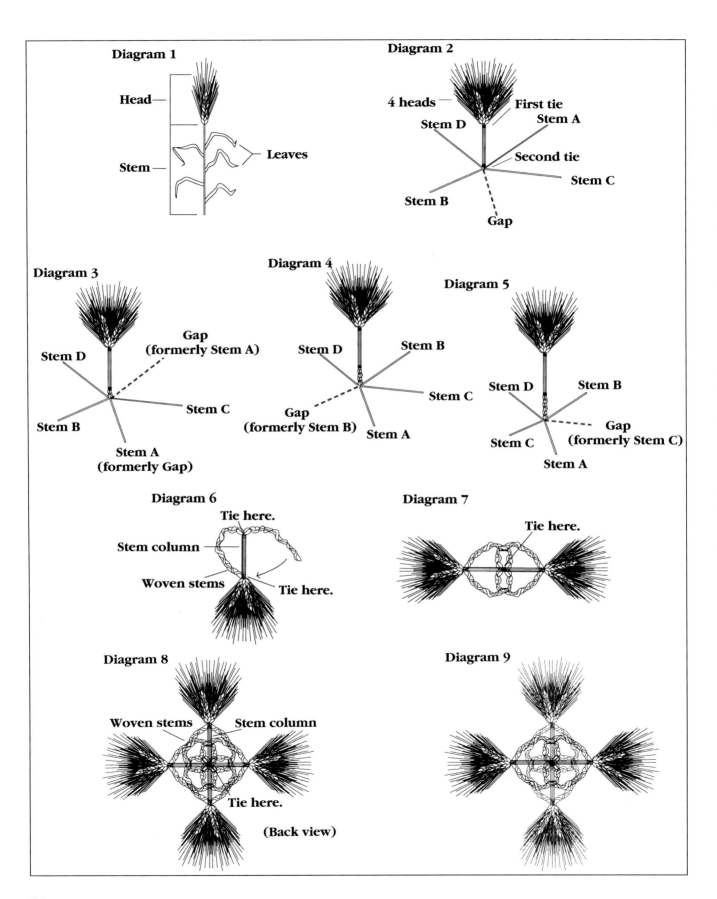

Diagram 1

Head

Stem

Leaves

Diagram 2

4 heads

First tie

Stem D

Stem A

Second tie

Stem C

Stem B

Gap

Diagram 3

Stem D

Gap
(formerly Stem A)

Stem C

Stem B

Stem A
(formerly Gap)

Diagram 4

Stem D

Stem B

Gap
(formerly Stem B)

Stem C

Stem A

Diagram 5

Stem D

Stem B

Stem C

Gap
(formerly Stem C)

Stem A

Diagram 6

Tie here.

Stem column

Woven stems

Tie here.

Diagram 7

Tie here.

Diagram 8

Woven stems

Stem column

Tie here.

(Back view)

Diagram 9

Above: Collector Sherry Phillips decorates her Christmas tree with a harvest of woven wheat ornaments. For information on how to order wheat weaving supplies, see source listing on page 154.

stem. When stem is spongy and bounces to the touch, it is ready; if it is still tough or brittle, soak it longer.) Keeping wheat wrapped in wet towel, pour out water.

To arrange stems for weaving, firmly tie 4 pieces of wheat together just below heads. Measuring 2″ from first tie, firmly tie again. Trim loose ends of threads.

Spreading stems out so that they are perpendicular to heads, grip wheat firmly at second tie with left hand. (Grip with right hand if left-handed.) Leaving a "gap," spread stems so that they are spaced as in Diagram 2. (Imagine a 5-pointed star with 1 point missing.)

Note: Practicing first with stems labeled A, B, C, and D will help you gain proficiency in the weaving technique.

To begin weaving, see Diagram 2 and move stem A into the gap. This step will form a gap in the A position. See Diagram 3 and move stem B into the former A position. See Diagram 4 and move stem C into the former B position. See Diagram 5 and move stem D into the former C position. (Always follow this sequence: A to gap, B to A, C to B, D to C.)

At the completion of each 4-stem weaving sequence, turn stems so that stem A is in its original position. Continue weaving in this manner until a 4″ section is completed. Using 4 new stems, repeat process.

When the second 4″ section is complete, tie the 2 (4-stem) groups together, with heads and stem ends aligned, at the 2 places at which each group is already tied. To hide any imperfections, pull woven stems gently to stretch.

Turn unit upside down, so that heads are at bottom. To form heart, pull each woven stem piece out and down to base of heads to make 1 lobe of heart shape. (See Diagram 6.) Tie ends of woven stem pieces at base of heads (where first tie was made) to form point of heart.

Repeat weaving instructions to make a second heart. Overlapping tops of hearts as shown in Diagram 7, tie them together at notch between lobes.

Make a second set of 2 hearts, repeating procedure used for first 2 hearts. (Do not tie bottom points at base of heads yet.)

Place the second set of 2 hearts underneath the first set of 2 hearts so that the center stem columns of the hearts form a cross shape. (See Diagram 8.) Tie all hearts together where stems intersect.

Pull the loose ends of the woven stems of second set of 2 hearts up and over lobes of first set of 2 hearts. To form points of hearts, tie loose ends of the woven stem pieces at base of heads. (See Diagram 9.)

To add fullness to the wreath, divide 28 stems evenly into 4 groups. Tie the groups at heads. Making sure the stem columns are aligned with the first set of stem columns, tie 1 group of stems behind each first set of heads to form a second stem cross. Trim excess stem ends so that only heads, woven hearts, and stem columns show. Tie the second stem cross underneath the stem cross of heart piece at heads and cross intersections.

Dry completed piece on a screen or rack to allow for proper air circulation.

The Magic of Candlelight

Nothing adds more warmth to holiday decorating than the magic of candlelight. Whether you group candle holders crafted by your own hands or from your prized collections, you'll create a feast of lights for your home.

Above: It's almost impossible to think of the holidays without the aroma of oranges, cloves, and cinnamon. For an eye-catching, yet simple, way to say "Christmas," stud oranges with whole cloves. Slice a small piece off the bottom so that orange will not roll over. Then cut a hole at the stem end to fit the candle. (Coating the hole and the sliced bottom with paraffin will prolong the life of the fruit.)

Above: A collection of frosted-glass chandelier lampshades is grouped for a radiant effect. (Turn the shade upside down on a mirror to make a cup holder for the candle.) Here, a purchased papier-mâché reindeer is the focal point of the centerpiece.

Right: The solid look of a bread wreath candle holder contrasted with graceful, tall, thin tapers is an unexpected combination. Shiny red apples, greenery, and ribbon complete this appealing centerpiece for an informal gathering.

Above: For natural candle holders, cut sections of a tree limb. With a three-quarter-inch drill bit, make a hole to fit a three-quarter-inch candle.

Left: Use your collection of faceted glassware as unusual candle holders. Here combined with a collection of plates, the grouping makes a sparkling holiday decoration.

Above: Antique inkwells used as candle holders lend the spirit of Christmas past to this striking holiday arrangement. Extend your own appreciation of history to the season by bringing out your collection of vintage treasures for candle holders.

Fabric Puff Wreaths

Right: Here's a way to use Christmas print fabric scraps to make candle holders: For each candle holder, cut ten small equal-size fabric circles. Run a line of gathering stitches near outside edge of circle. Place a small puff of stuffing or two cotton balls on wrong side of fabric. Gather fabric around puff and pull tightly to close. Take two or three stitches to secure. To make wreath, join puffs by running a thread through centers. Pull tightly to fit the candle. (For safety, place candle in a small, inconspicuous candle holder before adding fabric wreath.) Attach bow. The patchwork teddy adds personality to this charming arrangement. The completed fabric wreath also makes a clever package topper. Two or three on a large package are especially effective. Friends will love receiving several for candle holders or just one for a tree ornament.

Holiday Handiwork

BELIEVE IN THE MAGIC
OF CHRISTMAS

✠

A CHRISTMAS CARDIGAN

✠

DANCING THROUGH
THE HOLIDAYS

✠

A COLONIAL CHRISTMAS IN CROSS-STITCH

✠

PRAIRIE GARLANDS

✠

IDEAS: TRY STAMPING:
IT'S WORTH REPEATING

Angels and Stars Herald the Season

These celestial creations will make a heavenly addition to your Christmas theme. Plump stuffed wings added to old-fashioned rag dolls make a quaint choir of angels, and the unexpected combination of lace and tin provides a striking textural contrast for fanciful star ornaments.

Above: Arrange and pin finished angels on a craft-foam cone wrapped with a long strip of dark-green fabric. Fresh greenery completes the angel tree.

Precious Angels

Materials for 3 angels:
pattern on page 128
cardboard or plastic template material
graphite paper (to transfer pattern)
#2 pencil
¼ yard (45″-wide) unbleached muslin
polyester stuffing
dowel for stuffing tool
¼ yard (45″-wide) red-and-white print fabric
3 pieces (¾″ x 1½″) iron-on interfacing
1 yard lace edging of desired width for dress hem
3 yards (1/16″-wide) red ribbon for lace insert (optional), sash, and hanging loop
3 skeins embroidery floss for hair (in colors of choice)
2 yards red crochet cotton for lace insert (optional) and hair bows
embroidery needle
toothbrush
hair spray (optional)
fine-point permanent markers: brown, red
pink blusher
cotton swab
¾ yard (5/8″-wide) lace for halo
3 (½″) star-shaped gold sequins
3 gold seed beads

Transfer pattern to template material, including all markings. Cut out templates.

To make 1 angel, fold muslin in half and mark outline of angel on top layer. Stitch along outline through both layers, using 12 or more stitches per inch. Cut out angel, adding ¼″ seam allowance all around. Trim corners and clip inside curves almost to stitching line. Cut slit on back of angel where indicated on pattern. Turn.

Repeat procedure to mark, stitch, cut, and turn wings.

Stuff angel and wings, using dowel in hard-to-reach areas. Whipstitch slits closed. Stitch through all layers along stitching line between body and arms. Stitch wings through all layers down center line.

Mark and cut out dress. Following manufacturer's directions, fuse a piece of interfacing to wrong side of dress where indicated by shading on pattern. Trim interfacing from neckline opening. With right sides facing, fold dress in half along shoulder line. Stitch side seams. Turn. Stitch lace to bottom of dress, gathering top edge of lace, if necessary, to fit curve of dress. Weave ribbon or crochet cotton through top edge of lace, if desired.

Put dress on angel, turn under ¼″ on 1 side of back opening, and overlap edges. Slipstitch back edge closed. Cut a 12″ length of ribbon and tie around dress just below arms.

Cut a skein of embroidery floss at 1 end to make a bundle of 12″ lengths. Make 3 piles with 3 (12″) lengths in each pile. Braid to make pigtails. Center pigtails on top of head on seam line and sew to head with 1 strand of floss.

Cut 2 (6″) lengths of crochet cotton. Tie a bow ½″ above each end of braid. Unbraid pigtails below tie and cut ends of crochet cotton to desired length. Fluff ends of pigtails.

To make bangs, thread embroidery needle with 6 strands of floss. Across forehead, just below braid, make stitches as close together as possible without overlapping (5 or 6 loops). Cut loops and trim bangs evenly. Brush bangs with a toothbrush to fluff and separate strands. Spray lightly with hair spray, if desired, to hold flat and in place.

Mark eyes and mouth with pencil dots. Practice applying markers to a scrap of fabric before applying to angel. Color eyes and mouth with markers. With cotton swab, add a touch of blusher to each cheek.

For halo, gather length of lace along 1 edge and pull gathers tightly to make a circle of lace. Whipstitch cut ends together. Tack halo to back of head. For hanger, make a loop from 6″ of ribbon. Knot ends and tack to center back at neckline. Tack wings to back at shoulder level. Fold arms to center and tack hands together. Sew a star sequin and bead to hands. Repeat to make 2 more angels.

Tin Stars

Materials:
pattern on page 133
plastic template material
graphite paper (to transfer pattern)
#2 pencil
sheet of tin designed for pierced metalcraft
7″ duck-billed tin snips
piece of scrap wood
old screwdrivers: regular and Phillips-head
hammer
nail or ice pick
8″ (¹⁄₁₆″-wide) red ribbon or string

Transfer pattern to template material and cut out. Mark outline on tin sheet and cut out with tin snips. *Caution: Edges will be very sharp.*

Lightly draw free-form design on tin with pencil before using screwdrivers to tap designs. (Refer to photograph on page 25 for design examples.) Place star on wood scrap to protect work surface. Place tip of screwdriver on design line and gently tap with hammer. Move screwdriver along design and continue tapping until finished. (Different-sized screwdriver heads make a variety of effects; for instance, the tip of a Phillips-head screwdriver forms a perfect dot.)

For hanger, punch hole through star point with nail or ice pick. Thread with ribbon or string for hanging. Knot ends of hanger.

Lace Stars

Materials:
1″-wide scalloped edging lace
matching thread
spray starch (optional)
8″ (¹⁄₁₆″-wide) red ribbon

Cut a 5½″ length of lace. Sew cut ends of lace together with ¼″ seam. Leaving a hole in the center, gather straight edge and pull tightly to form star shape. Spray with water and press with warm iron so that star will lie flat. Spray with starch, if desired. Thread with ribbon for hanging. Knot ends of hanger.

Left: Let the joy of Christmas shine in everything you do this season. Add soft Lace Stars to a package wrap or glue Lace Stars to Tin Stars for unusual ornaments.

Believe in the Magic of Christmas

*Engelbreit's the name.
Cute is my game.*

One year Mary Engelbreit decided she had to make Christmas extra-special for her family in Webster Groves, Missouri. She and her husband and business partner, Philip Delano, were a little concerned over their seven-year-old son, Evan, and his sudden doubts about the existence of Santa Claus. So Mary, a gifted illustrator, put her artistic flair to work and began decorating early in the season. She went all out. She hung garlands everywhere and brought in a giant Christmas tree. It was quite impressive. But despite her efforts, Evan still looked skeptical.

Christmas Eve arrived, and what should have been a most sparkling day really looked a little withered. The problem was the Christmas tree. Weeks and weeks in the house had taken its toll on the poor evergreen. Evan and his younger brother, Will, went to sleep that night still wondering if there really was a Santa Claus.

The boys lost every doubt the next morning. There in the center of all their new Christmas-morning toys stood a fresh, green, newly decorated Christmas tree. It was plain that only Santa himself would have had the foresight to bring a whole new tree to their house.

Had the delighted boys been a little older, they'd have seen a hint of what Santa had in store in one of their mom's most famous Christmas illustrations. In her drawing, Santa is dressed in a sweeping, soft red robe, and he carries a bulging, star-spangled sack of toys. He stands on a roof looking down the chimney. Above him is one word in large red letters: BELIEVE.

About 12 years ago, Mary started drawing illustrations for a greeting card company in California. A self-taught artist, she had done commercial artwork for several years. In 1982, when she was pregnant with Will, she started her own card company and began fine-tuning her winsome style. She already had a following, thanks to her 1977 illustration, *Life is just a chair of bowlies,* which features a little girl holding a basket of cherries while admiring an overstuffed chair that is filled with multicolored bowls.

After only two years in business, another greeting card company, Sunrise Publications, made her an offer that was just right. Sunrise now licenses the use of her illustrations for cards sold internationally.

"Now I'm free to draw," Mary says. "They just send me a list of their greeting card needs—so many get well cards, so many birthday, so many Christmas. I work on them through the year."

Mary is also free to explore exciting new territory. A line of fabrics and children's clothes based on her illustrations will soon be on the market (from Daisy Kingdom in Portland, Oregon). But it's when she mentions her latest project that Mary really gets excited.

"The children's book!" Mary exclaims. "It's about a little girl getting her first pair of glasses," she says, as she adjusts her own. "I'm collaborating with a dear friend from grade school, Debby Busch. It's due out in the spring of 1991."

With so many projects to juggle, Mary stays busy year-round. It's in midsummer when she really steeps herself in Christmas.

"By July I really start to miss Christmas, so

Above: Mary and Phil work well together, whether for the business or the family. Their sons, Evan (standing) and Will, appear at different ages and stages in many of Mary's illustrations.

that's when I work on my holiday illustrations," Mary explains. "I get out all my old Christmas books, turn on the Christmas carols, and go to work."

When Mary tells the story of the magical appearance of the mystery Christmas tree, her love for her sons shines in her face. It's plain she and Philip will try to make every Christmas just as special.

She looks at this year's Christmas tree surrounded by scores of packages embellished with her own illustrations. There's a royally robed lion leading a tiny red-sweatered lamb. Across the bottom are the words: *Peace on Earth*. A

blonde, cherub-faced boy in red footed pajamas, his belly button winking out, shouts, "I Love Christmas!" Finally, of course, there's a big package with Santa on the front. The jolly old elf wears a flowing red robe and peers knowingly down the chimney. This one just might be a present for Evan.

Above: Mary's heartwarming, fun-loving artistic style can be seen in three dimensions in her home decorating. Cherries dance across the mantel to frame an Engelbreit motto: Be warm inside and out. She painted a boy-sized chair in bright colors for each son. Stockings, sold through the Mary Engelbreit company, wait to be filled. (For information on how to order stockings or other Mary Engelbreit designs, see source listing on page 154.)

Right: Since childhood, Mary has been a collector. These Christmas trees represent one of several collections, including reindeer and snowmen, that decorate Mary's home every day of the year.

Below: Another of Mary's collections: miniature chairs. She painted the jazzy yellow one.

Of her various collections, Mary says, "When I was a child, my mom and I would go out collecting things at antique places. Then we'd come home, move the furniture all around, and just drive everybody else crazy!"

Left: From trailing ivy to bright urns of sunflowers, Mary's front door gives ample invitation to the warmth and whimsy within.

Left: A favorite black-and-white checkerboard effect can be seen throughout Mary's work as well as her house. The fire screen is actually an old card table that "just happened to fit exactly." The charming wool appliqué pillow is a handmade gift from her friend Charlotte Lyons.

31

Mary Engelbreit's Painted Pillows

Mary shares two of her charming designs for holiday pillows.

Materials for 1 pillow:
pattern on page 136
12″ of string
thumbtack
#2 pencil
tracing paper
1 yard (45″-wide) white cotton sheeting
transfer pencil
posterboard
textile medium
acrylic paints (see pattern for colors)
fabric paintbrushes
embroidery floss: black, red, white
embroidery needle
1½ yards (⅛″-wide) ribbon for trim
14″ circular pillow form

Make a compass with string, thumbtack, and #2 pencil. (Leave 8″ of string free when tying to pencil.) Draw a 16″ circle on tracing paper.

From white fabric, cut 1 (10″ x 40″) strip for ruffle and 3 (16″) circles. Cut top ⅓ away from 2 of the circles. (Remaining ⅔ of these circles will make pillow back.) Fold whole paper circle in half, then into fourths. Open paper circle. Using fold lines as guides, center central design of pattern on paper circle and trace design. Position ¼ border pattern between 2 fold lines and trace. Move pattern to next quarter section of border and repeat to complete border.

Turn tracing over. Using transfer pencil, trace over all design and border lines.

With transfer-pencil side down, place tracing on right side of the whole fabric circle. Following manufacturer's instructions, use hot iron to transfer design to fabric.

Painting and Embroidering Design

For a smooth painting surface, lay fabric circle right side up on posterboard. Following manufacturer's instructions, mix textile medium with acrylic paints. Begin painting at the center of design and paint towards borders. Using tip of

paintbrush handle, make dots for snowflakes in both central designs. Let paint dry completely.

For embroidery detailing on snowman pillow, outline-stitch all outlines in central design with 2 strands of black floss. (See photograph.) Using 2 strands of black floss, work buttons and mouth with French knots. Using 2 strands of red floss, work holly berries with French knots. Using 2 strands of white floss, backstitch along outline of border snowflakes. Using 3 strands of black floss, outline-stitch outer and inner border circles.

For embroidery detailing on Santa pillow, outline-stitch facial features, beard, and fur on garments with 1 strand of black floss. Using 1 strand of black floss, work detail on fur trim on suit and cap with lazy daisy stitch. Using 2 strands of black floss, work checkerboard trim on suit and cap with satin stitches. Using 2 strands of black floss, outline-stitch all other details in central design. (See photograph.) Using 2 strands of red floss, work holly berries around inner border and on Santa's cap with French knots. Using 3 strands of black floss, outline-stitch outer border circle, including 4 leaves that extend beyond border.

Constructing Pillow

For pillow back, on the ⅔ circles, turn under ¼" twice along each straight edge and stitch hem. For ruffle, with right sides facing and raw edges aligned, stitch 10″ ends together to make 1 continuous circle. With wrong sides facing, fold ruffle in half lengthwise to make a 5″-wide doubled ruffle. Press fold. Divide into 4 equal parts and mark with pins. Run a gathering thread along raw edge. Pull thread to gather.

Divide pillow front into quarters. With right sides facing and raw edges aligned, pin ruffle to pillow front, matching quarter marks and adjusting gathers to fit. Using ½″ seam, baste ruffle to pillow front.

For pillow back, overlap hemmed edges on back pieces until back circle matches front and pin. With right sides facing, pin back pieces to front. Using ½″ seam, stitch around circle through all layers. Trim seams and clip curves. Turn and press.

Leaving tails of equal length at beginning and end, stitch ribbon trim to fabric at inside edge of ruffle. Tie ends of ribbon in a bow. Insert pillow form.

A Christmas Cardigan

This comfortable sweater is made from three colors of standard four-ply worsted-weight acrylic yarn. The stitch-from-the-top-down directions allow you to custom-size the garment and knit a perfect fit for any child. Some experience in knitting is necessary, but this is not a difficult project.

Materials:
4-ply worsted-weight acrylic yarn (230-yard skeins): 1 (2, 2, 2) skeins white, 1 (1, 1, 2) skeins Christmas ombre stripe, 1 (1, 2, 2) skeins red
sizes 5 and 8 (24″ or 29″) circular knitting needles, or size to obtain gauge
2 smaller-size circular knitting needles and rubber point-protectors for stitch holders
stitch markers
tapestry needle
size D crochet hook
7 (¾″-diameter) plastic rings

Note: Standard Knitting Abbreviations are on page 153.

SIZES: Directions are for small size (chest measurement of 21″). Changes for medium size (chest measurement of 23″), large size (chest measurement of 26″), and extra-large size (chest measurement of 29″) are in parentheses.

GAUGE: 5 sts = 1″ in St st on larger needles.

Note: Sweater is k from the top down in 1 piece. Sweater can be fitted to wearer as it is being k by sl as if to p some of the sts to a smaller-size circular needle and putting point-protectors on ends of needles. Lay piece over shoulders of wearer. If sweater is wide enough but not long enough, work a few extra rows even. If it is long enough but not wide enough, cast on extra sts at the underarm.

SWEATER: Starting at neck edge, with larger needles and white yarn, cast on 1 (1, 1, 1) st for right front, sl marker on needle to mark sleeve edge, cast on 6 (8, 10, 12) sts for right sleeve, add marker, cast on 21 (23, 23, 25) sts for back, add marker, cast on 6 (8, 10, 12) sts for left sleeve, add marker, cast on 1 (1, 1, 1) st for left front. A total of 35 (41, 45, 51) sts have been cast on.

Row 1: P. *Row 2:* Inc before and after each marker as follows: inc in first st by k into front and back of st, * sl marker, inc in next st as before, k to within 1 st of next marker, inc as before, rep from * 2 times more, end with sl marker, inc in last st [43 (49, 53, 59) sts]. *Row 3:* P. *Row 4:* Inc in first st, before and after each marker, and in last st as follows: * inc, k to within 1 st of marker, inc, sl marker, rep from * 3 times more, end with inc, k to last st, inc [53 (59, 63, 69) sts]. *Row 5:* P. *Row 6:* Inc in first st, before and after each marker, and in next to last st [63 (69, 73, 79) sts]. Rep rows 5 and 6, 2 (3, 3, 4) times more, to make a total of 5 (6, 6, 7) inc. [A total of 83 (89, 93, 99) sts after last row 6 rep.] At end of last row 6 rep, cast on 2 (3, 3, 3) sts more. At end of next p row, cast on 2 (3, 3, 3) sts more to complete neck shaping. Continue working in St st inc before and after each marker. When center back length measures 3″ (or desired length), change to Christmas ombre yarn on p row. Continue as before until there are 53 (59, 65, 73) sts across back and center back length measures 4½″ (5″, 6″, 7″).

Divide for sleeves and body: With wrong side facing and small ball of ombre yarn, work across front sts to first marker. Sl these sts as if to p to another circular needle. In same manner, sl sts for other half of front to opposite end of this same needle, putting point-protectors on ends of needle. Join 2nd ball of ombre yarn and work across sleeve sts to next marker. Join 3rd ball of ombre yarn and work across back sts to next sleeve marker. Sl back sts as before to 3rd circular needle and secure ends. Join 4th ball of ombre yarn and work across rem sleeve sts.

SLEEVES: Continue to work both sleeves in St st at same time on same needle with separate balls of yarn. Cast on 2 sts at each edge of each sleeve on next 2 rows. Work sleeves even for 1″, ending after p row. *Next row:* K 1, k 2 tog tbl, k to last 3 sts, k 2 tog, k 1. Rep dec every 3rd k row 4 (5, 6, 7) times more. Work even until sleeves measure 8″ (9½″, 11″, 13″) long from body [or 1½″ (2″, 2″, 2″) less than desired length], end after p row. Change to smaller needles, join red, and k 1 row. * P 1, p 2 tog, rep from * across, adjusting as necessary to end row

with odd number of sts on needle. Work in k 1, p 1 ribbing for 1½″ (2″, 2″, 2″). Bind off loosely in rib pat.

BODY: With wrong side facing, sl sts for left front onto larger needles. Join small ball of ombre yarn and cast on 4 sts. P across front. Turn and k back across these front sts, then k underarm and back sts. Cast on 4 sts for other underarm and k across rem front. Work even in St st on entire body until piece measures 8″ (9″, 10″, 11″) from underarm [or 2″ (2½″, 3″, 3″) less than desired length], end after p row. Change to smaller needles, join red, and k 1 row. Work in p 1, k 1, ribbing for 2″ (2½″, 3″, 3″). Bind off loosely in rib pat.

COLLAR: With right side facing, smaller needles, and red yarn, pick up and k 6 (9, 9, 10) sts on front, 1 st in every st across sleeve, back, and rem sleeve, and 6 (9, 9, 10) sts on rem front. K across row working 1 inc in each st, adjusting as necessary to end row with even number of sts on needle. Then work even in Brioche rib for 3″ as follows: *Row 1:* * Yo, sl 1, k 1, rep from * across. *Row 2:* * Yo, sl 1, k 2 tog (sl st and yo of previous row), rep from * across. Rep row 2 only for 3″. Bind off loosely.

FRONT BANDS: With safety pins, mark appropriate buttonhole placement on front (right for girls, left for boys). With right side facing, smaller needles, and red yarn, pick up sts along front edge in 3 rows out of 4. Work even in k 1, p 1 ribbing for ½″. Work buttonholes over 2 rows as follows: *First row:* Bind off 2 sts for each buttonhole. *Next row:* Cast on 2 sts above 2 bind-offs for each buttonhole. Work even ½″ more in rib pat. Bind off loosely in rib pat. Pick up sts along rem front edge as before. Work even in k 1, p 1 ribbing for 1¼″. Bind off loosely in rib pat.

FINISHING: Sew sleeve seams.

BUTTONS: With crochet hook and red yarn, place loop on hook, leaving 15″ tail of yarn. Work as many single crochet stitches as possible around ring. Cut yarn, leaving 15″ tail, and pull tail through last single crochet. Thread tail of yarn into tapestry needle and make overcast stitch in the outside loop of every other single crochet stitch. Pull thread tightly to draw all stitches to back of button. Secure the center of the button with some stitches. Use both yarn ends to attach button to sweater. Repeat for other buttons.

Dancing Through The Holidays

Early needleworkers favored the red-on-white stitching featured in this joyful design.

Dancing Children Pillow Cover

Materials:
pattern on page 134
2 yards (45"-wide) muslin
graphite paper (to transfer pattern)
#2 pencil
embroidery hoop
1 skein red embroidery floss
embroidery needle
¼ yard (45"-wide) red-and-white cotton print
thread to match
2 yards (¼"-wide) cotton cording
¾ yard (45"-wide) solid red cotton
6 (¾") flat red buttons
12" x 16" pillow

Note: All seam allowances are ½". To make a cover for any pillow size, cut muslin 2" wider and 8" longer than pillow. Adjust cording and ruffle accordingly.

Cut 3 (17½" x 26") pieces from muslin. Centering embroidery design, transfer design onto right side of 1 muslin piece. Using embroidery hoop to hold fabric taut and using 3 strands of floss, outline-stitch along all transferred lines. (Do not carry floss on wrong side of fabric, or floss will show through.)

To line embroidered panel, with right sides facing, lay 1 muslin piece on embroidered panel. Baste muslin to embroidered panel at ends. Turn. With right sides facing, pin remaining muslin piece to embroidered pillow top. Using

Opposite: Visions of sugarplums are sure to dance in the dreams of the child who naps on this pillow. (Photographed in the bed-and-breakfast cottage of Pete and Donna Steffen of Cedarburg, Wisconsin.)

Above: The children appear to hold hands as they dance in a circle around the tree. To achieve this effect, simply reverse the design on alternating panels.

½" seam and leaving both ends open, stitch along top and bottom of pillow top through all layers to make a tube.

For piping, cut 2"-wide bias strips from print fabric, piecing as needed to equal 2 yards. Make 2 yards of corded piping. Cut piping in half. With right sides facing and raw edges aligned, pin 1 piece of piping around 1 end of tube. Using zipper foot, baste piping to tube along stitching line of piping. Repeat for other end.

For ruffle, cut 6½"-wide bias strips from red fabric, piecing as needed to equal 2¾ yards. Cut in half widthwise. With wrong sides facing and raw edges aligned, fold 1 bias strip in half lengthwise. Press. Run a gathering thread along long raw edge. Pull to fit around 1 end of tube. With right sides facing and raw edges aligned, pin ruffle around tube. Stitch along stitching line of piping. Trim seam to ¼". Finish raw edges with zigzag or overcast stitch. Repeat with remaining strip on other end of tube. Turn.

On each end of pillow top, mark 3 (1") evenly spaced buttonholes 2" from piping. Work buttonholes. Sew buttons opposite buttonholes on inside of pillow back. Insert pillow.

Dancing Children Tree Skirt

Materials:
pattern and placement diagram on page 134
several sheets of tissue paper
#2 pencil
30″ of string
pushpin or thumbtack
7 yards (45″-wide) muslin
graphite paper (to transfer pattern)
embroidery hoop
6 skeins red embroidery floss
embroidery needle
1 twin-size quilt batting
⅔ yard (45″-wide) red-and-white cotton
  print
thread to match
5 yards (¼″) cotton cording
1½ yards (45″-wide) solid red cotton

Note: All seam allowances are ½″.

Tape several sheets of tissue paper together to make a 60″ square. Mark center of square with a pencil dot. Fold square in half, then into fourths. Now fold on diagonal, with folded edges together. To make circle, attach string to tissue at dot with pushpin. Measure 27″ of string and tie remaining string to pencil to make a compass. Holding string taut, draw an arc with a 27″ radius on the folded tissue. To make center circle, draw an arc with a 2½″ radius in same manner. Cut out both circles along marked lines. (See Diagram.) Unfold tissue. Cut along 2 adjacent fold lines on tissue to make pattern for 1 tree skirt panel. Pin pattern to muslin. Adding ½″

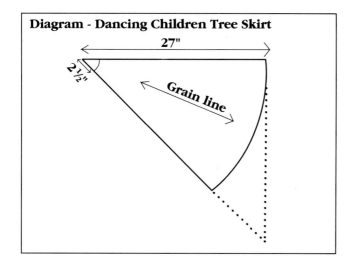

Diagram - Dancing Children Tree Skirt

27″

2½″

Grain line

seam allowance all around, cut 16 panels from muslin. Set aside 8 panels for backing.

Centering embroidery pattern 3″ from bottom edge, transfer design to right side of 4 panels. Reverse pattern and transfer design to right side of remaining 4 panels. Using embroidery hoop to hold fabric taut and using 3 strands of embroidery floss, outline-stitch along all transferred lines. (Do not carry floss on wrong side of fabric, or floss will show through.)

For skirt top, with right sides facing, stitch alternating embroidered panels together along side seams, leaving first and last panels unjoined. (See photograph on page 37.) Stitch 8 plain panels together in same manner for backing. Using backing as a pattern, cut a circle from batting. Press embroidered top and backing with warm iron, pressing seams to 1 side.

Cut 2″-wide bias strips from print fabric, piecing as needed to equal 5 yards. Make 5 yards of corded piping. With right sides facing and raw edges aligned, pin piping to outside edge of skirt. Using zipper foot, baste piping to skirt, stitching along stitching line of piping.

For ruffle, cut 6½″-wide bias strips from red fabric, piecing as needed to equal 4⅛ yards. With wrong sides facing and raw edges aligned, fold strip in half lengthwise. Press. Gather strip along raw edge to fit skirt top. With right sides facing and raw edges aligned, baste ruffle to skirt top along stitching line of piping.

For ties, cut 2 (2″ x 15″) strips from print. Press under ½″ along both long sides and on 1 end of each strip. Fold each strip in half lengthwise. Topstitch close to all edges. With right sides facing and raw edges aligned, baste 1 tie each at midpoint on outer straight edge of first and last panel of skirt top. Stack in this order: batting, backing (right side up), and skirt top (right side down). Pin edges together, securing all layers. Leaving center circle open for turning, stitch remaining edges through all layers. Clip curves. Turn. Baste edges of center circle together. Clip curves. Press skirt.

To bind center circle, cut 2″-wide bias strips from print, piecing as needed to measure 1¼ yards. With right sides facing and raw edges aligned, pin strip on center circle so that a 14″ tail extends beyond each side for ties. Stitch. Fold strip to back of skirt, turn under ½″ seam allowance on raw edges, and slipstitch to backing. Topstitch ties close to edges.

A Colonial
Christmas in Cross-Stitch

*Cross-stitch designer Sandra Sullivan makes
a festive switch of stitchery to deck the halls of
her colonial-style home for the season.*

Above: The Sullivan's colonial-style family room is a warm and inviting place any time of the year, but especially during the holidays. The rich brick-red trim of the shuttered window, paneled fireplace, and crown moldings is colorful accompaniment to holiday greenery and Sandra's cross-stitchery. The Christmas pillow nestled in the chair at right is Sandra's design—she shares her instructions on page 42.

Left: In this welcoming vignette, a seasonal exchange of stitchery and a feather tree signal Christmastime. Cross-stitched Santas make an appearance in a small scene with a bear and a tree and as the O in a welcome hanging.

Sandra Sullivan started doing needlework in college. Even then she was drawn to a traditional style and, after she married, she sought colonial and country needlework patterns to accessorize her furnishings. Not finding any, she decided to try designing her own.

Although Sandra enjoyed various needle arts, especially crewel and needlepoint, "I knew immediately when I first read about cross-stitch that it was for me," she says. This simple technique, which could show intricate detail, offered Sandra the perfect medium through which to develop her own designs in the style she loved.

When Sandra took her original designs to a needlework and frame shop for finishing, the owner encouraged her to chart her work to sell to others. Sandra heeded that advice—she has since published more than 100 leaflets and has her own shop, Homespun Elegance, in Fredericksburg, Virginia.

In her home today, Sandra's cross-stitch is attractively integrated into her colonial-style decor year-round. And come the holidays, she pulls out her Christmas cross-stitch to place throughout the house. In addition to decorating a big tree and several feather trees with ornaments and scattering holiday pillows around, she also replaces some wall hangings with festive stitchery just for the season.

This year, you may want to consider Sandra's approach to holiday decorating for your home. A seasonal exchange of accessories assures a fresh and festive look for familiar settings.

Above: A feather tree in the foyer is decorated with Sandra's fringed mini-sampler ornaments. The floral stitchery atop the mirror, a charming year-round application of cross-stitch, is also Sandra's handiwork.

40

Below: In a homey downstairs den, the Sullivans' big Christmas tree is graced with lots of cross-stitched ornaments. Beneath the boughs is a menagerie of country toys. Sandra's Santa pillow stands on a drop-leaf table. In a close look at the tree at left, you'll see an ornament (a Santa in an S), one of Sandra's Christmas-letter designs offered on the following pages.

Letter-Perfect Cross-Stitchery

Sandra illustrated the letters of C-H-R-I-S-T-M-A-S in cross-stitch—a versatile design that can be stitched in one piece for a chair back pillow, below opposite, or letter by letter for a garland or individual ornaments, above.

Materials for 1 ornament:
chart and color key on page 140
6½″ x 7¼″ unbleached 27-count brown linen
embroidery floss (see color key)
embroidery needle
mild soap
3¾″ x 4½″ coordinating fabric for backing
polyester stuffing
thread to match linen
embroidery floss to match border

Using 2 strands of floss over 2 threads, begin stitching at center of design. Follow chart to complete design.

Using mild soap, wash design piece in cold water. Rinse thoroughly. Roll in terry-cloth towel to remove excess water. Place stitched side down on dry terry-cloth towel; press with hot iron. (Do not use steam.) Allow to dry. Trim design piece to 3¾″ x 4½″. With right sides facing, pin backing to design piece.

Using ¼″ seam and leaving 1½″ opening on bottom edge, stitch around ornament. Trim corners and turn. Stuff loosely. Slipstitch opening closed.

For hanger, cut 6 (8″) lengths of 6-strand floss. Holding the 6 lengths together, tie a knot ¼″ from 1 end. Divide lengths into 3 equal parts and braid. Knot ¼″ from end and trim ends evenly. Using matching floss, tack knots to top corners of ornament.

Materials for pillow:
chart and color key on page 140
10″ x 19″ (27-count) cream linen
embroidery floss (see color key)
embroidery needle
mild soap
½ yard (45″-wide) coordinating fabric for back and border
#2 pencil
polyester stuffing
thread to match linen
1 yard (⅛″-wide) coordinating satin ribbon for bows
1 yard (¼″-wide) coordinating satin ribbon for hangers (optional)

Center and mark 10 (3″) squares (5 across by 2 down) on linen. Using 2 strands DMC 422 over 2 threads, cross-stitch blocks for letters. (See photograph.) Omitting borders on chart, center letters within blocks and follow chart to complete design. Use dated diamond design for tenth block. Using mild soap, wash design piece in cold water. Rinse thoroughly. Roll in terrycloth towel to remove excess water. Place stitched side down on dry towel; press with hot iron. (Do not use steam.) Allow to dry.

Trim linen 1″ from block border.

For borders, from coordinating fabric, cut 2 (3″ x 12″) strips for sides and 2 (3″ x 20½″) strips for top and bottom. Mark center on 1 long edge of each border strip and each edge of design piece. With right sides facing, raw edges aligned, and center marks matching, stitch border strips to design piece with ¼″ seam, stitching to within ¼″ of each corner and then taking 2 or 3 backstitches. Press seams toward border.

To miter corners, fold right sides of 2 adjacent strips together and sew at a 45-degree angle. (See Diagram.) Trim seam allowance to ¼″. Repeat for remaining corners.

For back, from remaining coordinating fabric, cut a piece the size of bordered pillow front. With right sides facing and raw edges aligned, stitch pillow front and back together with ½″ seam, leaving 6″ opening. Clip corners, turn, and press.

Shape polyester stuffing into soft rolls. With design right side up, lightly stuff border area

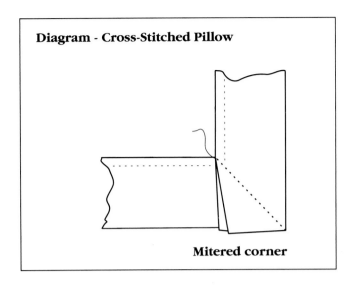

Diagram - Cross-Stitched Pillow

Mitered corner

except at opening. Pin design piece to backing along seam where border joins linen. Topstitch through all layers along this seam, leaving a 6″ opening above first opening. Stuff center of pillow with stuffing. Topstitch along opening at border/linen seam line. Finish stuffing border. Slipstitch opening closed.

Cut 4 (9″) lengths of ⅛″-wide ribbon. Fold each ribbon in half and tack 1 fold to each corner of design piece. Tie into bows. Cut 2 (18″) lengths of ¼″-wide ribbon for hangers, if desired. Fold each ribbon in half and tack folds to back of pillow at top corners.

Santa Steps Out in Checks and Plaids

Our tall wooden Santa does not have an ample tummy, but the original Saint Nicholas was, in fact, tall, thin, and stately. Here he's all dressed up in checks for holiday fun. And our roly-poly little fellow in his plaid suit waits happily for the big day, arms open in anticipation. He's easy to make . . . and easy to love.

Checkered Santa

Materials:
pattern on page 147
tracing paper
#2 pencil
10″ (1½″ x 1½″) pine
band saw or tabletop scroll saw
fine-toothed blades for saw
medium- and fine-grade sandpaper
small C-clamp
small scrap of wood
carving tool with 1 straight and 1 curved blade
acrylic paints: white, red, burnt umber
paintbrushes: ½″ and ¼″ square shader brushes
liquid dishwashing detergent
black fine-tip permanent marker

Transfer all markings for side view of pattern onto wood. Using fine-toothed blade, cut out shape with band saw or tabletop scroll saw. Turn wood a quarter turn so that Santa is face up. Transfer all markings for front view onto wood and cut out to shape top of head.

Using medium-grade sandpaper, round all edges except bottom.

Clamp wood to work surface with small C-clamp. To protect wood surface, place small scrap of wood between clamp and Santa.

To carve top edge of brim of Santa's hat, fit straight blade into carving tool. Holding blade perpendicular to Santa, insert it ⅛″ into wood. Pull blade out of wood and insert it again, abutting the first incision so that there will be an unbroken incised line. (*Note:* For safety, always

Above: Not the usual plump and jolly old elf, this slim little fellow has a stately presence all his own.

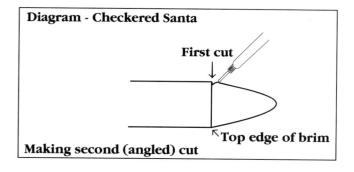

Diagram - Checkered Santa

First cut

Top edge of brim

Making second (angled) cut

cut away from yourself and keep both hands behind blade at all times.) Continue around 4 sides of hat. Each time you turn wood, be sure to place small scrap of wood between clamp and Santa.

When incised line is complete, place blade at a slight angle ⅜″ from incised line to make second cut. (See Diagram.) Slowly push blade into wood until it meets first cut. Remove thin wedge of wood. Repeat around top of brim.

Repeat procedure to carve bottom edge of brim around sides and back of Santa, except approach from below brim.

Following perpendicular cut/angle cut technique, carve along all facial lines and beard. Just under bottom edge of beard, carve away excess wood, making body slightly concave to about ½″ below edge of beard. With curved blade, round all edges except bottom of beard. Sand well with fine sandpaper.

Using ½″ paintbrush, paint beard, mustache, and edges of hair white. Let dry ½ hour. (Clean paintbrush with liquid dishwashing detergent, rinse thoroughly, and dry between colors.) Using ½″ paintbrush, paint hat and robe red. Let dry ½ hour. Experiment with checkerboard pattern on scrap wood before painting pattern on robe. Using ¼″ paintbrush, dab white squares in a checkerboard design on robe, leaving a solid band of red down the center front and around bottom. Experiment with a mixture of white, red, and burnt umber to make peach color for face. Using same paintbrush, paint face and let dry ½ hour. Using same paintbrush, paint whites of eyes and let dry ½ hour. With black marker, draw a very fine outline around bottom of eyes and fill in pupils.

Below: Roly-Poly Santa is full of birdseed and has quite an appetite for festivities. Several Roly-Poly Santas grouped with Checkered Santa companions will add a humorous note to the season.

Roly-Poly Santa

Materials:
pattern on page 132, photo on page 45
tracing paper
¼ yard (45″-wide) red-and-white plaid
¼ yard (45″-wide) muslin
⅛ yard white polar fleece or flannel
12″ crepe-wool hair
small plastic sandwich bag
¾ cup birdseed
polyester stuffing
white glue
2 (⅜″) buttons
1 small jingle bell
black embroidery floss
pink powdered blush
cotton swab

Note: For information on how to order crepe-wool hair, see source listing on page 154.

Transfer patterns to tracing paper, including markings. Pin patterns to fabric and cut out pieces as indicated.

Run a gathering thread ¼″ from edge of body piece. Fill bag with birdseed and place in center of circle. Pull thread to gather, adding stuffing as necessary to fill in around bag of seed. Leave a dime-size opening in top of body and tie off. Run a gathering thread ¼″ from edge of each hand piece. Pull thread to gather and stuff. Wrap thread tightly around gathers and tie off.

With right sides facing, fold sleeve as indicated on pattern and stitch along long edge. Turn. Turn under ¼″ on each end and press. Run a gathering thread around edge on 1 end of sleeve. Place gathered edge of hand inside gathered edge of sleeve and pull thread to gather tightly. Sew hand to sleeve. Stuff sleeve lightly. Repeat for other sleeve. Sew arms to top of body at opening on opposite sides.

Run a gathering thread ¼″ from edge of head piece. Pull thread to gather and stuff head firmly. Wrap thread tightly around gathers and tie off. Tuck gathered edge of head inside body opening and tack to secure.

With right sides facing, sew hat pieces together, leaving bottom open. Clip curves, turn, and press. Stuff lightly. Place hat on head and tack in place.

Glue hatband to head around bottom edge of hat, overlapping end at back of hat. Glue collar in place around Santa's neck, with edges meeting in front. Glue buttons in place on front of Santa's body. Glue bell to tip of hat.

With 2 strands of black floss, sew French knots for eyes. Glue beard to face, beginning at 1 edge of hatband, curving down around face, and ending at other edge of hatband. Apply blush to cheeks with cotton swab.

A Bit of Santa Lore

When we think of Santa Claus today, the image that comes immediately to mind is of a chubby man dressed in red, with twinkling blue eyes and a jolly "ho, ho, ho." For hundreds of years, however, Europeans imagined Saint Nicholas as tall, thin, and stately. This version of Saint Nick came from the fourth century, when the tall and slender bishop of Myra went among the poor with gifts.

In 1809, American writer Washington Irving published *Knickerbocker's History of New York*, in which he created a jolly creature who looked very much like a Dutch settler. In 1822, Clement C. Moore continued Santa's new look in his poem "A Visit from St. Nicholas."

Thomas Nast, the famous American cartoonist, further developed the figure of the Christmas saint, by then called Santa Claus, in a cartoon in 1863. In 1866, his drawing *Santa Claus and His Works* appeared in *Harper's Weekly*.

In 1931, artist Haddon Sundblom added a final touch to America's image of Santa. His painting for a Coca-Cola advertisement soon became the accepted portrait of Santa Claus.

Santa Claus's Mail
by Thomas Nast

Prairie Garlands

Oftentimes, the simplest designs are the most charming. And this description definitely fits these 2 easy-to-make prairie garlands. The fresh appeal of the pair comes from a country look blended with contemporary colors.

The triangle garland is an adaptation of the traditional prairie-point quilt edging. For your prairie-point garland, gather small amounts of assorted cotton print fabrics. The only additional supplies you'll need are the pattern on page 147, single-sided medium-weight fusible interfacing, and matching thread.

You'll find it easier to fuse the interfacing to the wrong side of the fabric before transferring the pattern and cutting out the triangles. After fusing and cutting, place 2 triangles with right sides facing. Stitch ¼″ from raw edge, leaving seam open between dots. Trim the corners, turn, and slipstitch opening closed.

To assemble garland, connect the triangles by running sewing thread between layers of fabric from center of base to tip. (See photograph.) The linked triangles give the effect of perky little Christmas trees perched along the branches.

The braided garland is even easier. A solid fabric, such as muslin, and 2 print fabrics work well together. Or, mix and match to your own taste. Because fabric shortens to about half its original length when braided, you'll need about twice as much fabric as you want the length of your finished braid to be.

Cut fabric into 4″-wide strips. For each strip, fold 1″ on long edges to wrong side and press. Fold in half to conceal raw edges. Anchor ends of 3 strips and braid. After braiding, secure ends by tucking under raw edges and slipstitching. Slipstitch ends of braids together to make 1 long garland.

An interesting variation is a chunky garland, made by braiding 3 single braids. This garland is especially effective on a mantel, hutch, or table.

Adapt a Coverlet Design

Cross-stitch a woven coverlet design to give Christmas trimmings a look of yesterday. With the ease of cross-stitch, this adaptation of an old-time weaving pattern works up quickly.

Woven coverlets were especially popular in 19th-century America. Sometimes the designs, many of which were brought from Europe, were purely geometric, but intricate floral and patriotic motifs were also widely used. The simple geometric motifs used here will lend your home a touch of Americana.

Coverlet Ornaments

Materials for 1 ornament:
chart on page 130 (refer to star on Coverlet Stocking chart)
2 (5″) squares of 28-count natural Irish linen
embroidery needle
embroidery floss: DMC 319, 321, or 783
table knife
9″ craft-foam ball
glue
3 (10″) pieces of ¼″-wide Cluny lace
10″ (⅜″-wide) ribbon to match floss
1 small gold-colored nail

Following stocking chart, center and cross-stitch 1 star design on 1 linen square for ornament front. (If you wish, cross-stitch design on second linen square for ornament back.) Trim squares to 5″ circles.

With table knife, run score line ¼″-deep around middle of foam ball. Center cross-stitched piece on half of ball. With knife, push edges of linen circle into the score line, smoothing cloth as you go. Repeat procedure to cover back of ornament, using remaining linen circle.

Glue 1 piece of lace along each long edge of ribbon. Let dry. Run bead of glue around score line on ornament. Beginning at top of ornament, glue lace-trimmed ribbon over score line around ornament, being sure to cover any rough edges. Turn under excess ribbon, overlap ends at top

of ornament, and glue end of ribbon in place. Set aside to dry.

For hanger, make loop with remaining piece of lace. Overlap ends and glue to top of ornament. Stick nail through overlapping ends of ribbon and lace to secure.

Coverlet Stocking

Materials:
chart, color key, and pattern on page 130
2 (14″ x 25″) pieces of 28-count natural Irish linen
fabric marker
embroidery floss (see color key)
embroidery needle
thread to match linen
1¾ yards of red piping
5″ (⅜″-wide) red grosgrain ribbon

Extend top of stocking pattern 5½″ for back and 9¾″ for front. Cut out. For stocking front, center pattern on 1 piece of linen and trace. Mark fold lines as shown on chart. Do not cut out stocking front. For stocking back, cut 1 stocking from remaining piece of linen, adding ½″ seam allowance all around, and set aside.

Stitching over 2 threads, begin by stitching toe design on stocking front, followed by pinecones, heel pattern, small diamonds, star pattern, large diamonds, and row of trees. Turn stocking front over, and center and stitch cuff design on wrong side of fabric between fold lines.

Adding ½″ seam allowance to sides and bottom edges, cut out stocking front.

Turn top edge under ½″ along first fold line and press. Turn cuff along second fold line down over right side of stocking front so that right side of design on cuff is showing. Press again.

With raw edges aligned and leaving a 1″ tail at beginning and ending of piping, baste piping to sides and bottom of stocking front. Turn tails to wrong side of stocking and tack to seam allowance.

Turn under ½″ at top of stocking back and press. With right sides facing and raw edges aligned, stitch stocking front to back around sides and bottom of stocking. Clip curves and turn stocking right side out. Place stocking right side down on terry-cloth towel. Press again.

For hanger, fold ribbon in half, and tack ends securely to seam allowance on inside right corner of stocking.

Little Miss Peep And Her Sheep

Charming Miss Peep and her wandering flock will settle down to celebrate Christmas morn with an appreciative child. Decked in her finest, from pantalets to pinafore, Bo has made sure she won't lose her soft white (fully jointed) sheep again. (Each of their bright-red neck ribbons sports a shining jingle bell!)

Bo Peep

Materials:
pattern on page 138
tracing paper
¼ yard (45″-wide) unbleached muslin
¼ yard (45″-wide) red miniprint
1 yard (45″-wide) lightweight white cotton fabric
water-soluble marker
acrylic paints: red, black, blue, brown, white
small paintbrush
sewing thread: off-white, yellow, red, white
polyester stuffing
1 skein pale yellow fingering-weight yarn
1 yard (⅛″-wide) red ribbon
2 yards (⅞″-wide) double-bound gathered white eyelet trim
40½″ (1″-wide) pleated white eyelet trim
37″ (½″-wide) flat white lace
1 small snap
compass
4 small white heart-shaped buttons
14″ of thin round elastic
tiny safety pin
wire clothes hanger
wire cutters
pliers
newspaper
cellophane tape
brown florists' tape
small bunch of artificial holly

Note: All seams are ¼″ unless otherwise noted.

Transfer patterns to tracing paper. Pin pattern pieces to fabric and cut out as indicated. Transfer all pattern markings to fabric with the water-soluble marker.

To make doll, paint facial features and boots, following pattern. Mix red and white paints to make pink for cheeks and mouth. Let pieces dry thoroughly before continuing.

On wrong side of fabric, sew darts in neck and tie off. With right sides facing, sew 2 leg pieces, leaving top open. Clip curves and turn. Repeat for other leg. With right sides facing, sew 2 arm pieces, leaving opening as indicated on pattern. Clip curves and turn. Repeat for other arm. Stuff arms lightly in hand area, more firmly around elbow, and lightly again near opening.

Machine-stitch between fingers as indicated on pattern. Stuff legs firmly to within 1″ of the opening.

Machine-stitch arms to right side of body front where indicated, with raw edges aligned and hands toward center. Machine-stitch legs to right side of body front where indicated, with raw edges aligned and feet toward head. With right sides facing and limbs tucked inside, sew body front to body back, leaving bottom edge open for turning. Clip neck and curves and turn.

Stuff body firmly. Turn under ¼″ on edges of opening and slipstitch closed with doubled thread.

For hair, cut yellow yarn into 15″ lengths. Lightly draw a line from the center of the forehead at the hairline, over the top of the head and down the center back of the head, ending at the top of the center dart. Center several strands of yellow yarn along hairline in center of forehead. Backstitch over yarn with matching thread to secure. Repeat until hair is secured to head all along the center line.

On both sides of face, loosely braid the front ½″ of hair, from center line as far as Xs. With yellow sewing thread, wrap hair just below braids and tack to head on side seams at Xs. Braid remainder of hair below Xs. Cut 2 (8″) lengths of red ribbon. Tie a bow around each braid. Fluff ends of braids.

To make skirt, cut a 7″ x 24″ rectangle from red miniprint. With right sides facing, fold in half widthwise to measure 7″ x 12″. Stitch ends together, leaving 1½″ of seam unstitched at top. Press seam allowance open. Topstitch close to edges to hem seam opening.

To hem skirt, cut 24″ of double-bound gathered eyelet trim. Sandwich bottom raw edge of skirt between the 2 layers of trim binding and sew with white thread, overlapping ends of trim ¼″ at back skirt seam.

To make decorative fold that covers binding on eyelet, fold eyelet trim to wrong side of skirt, with fold line of skirt fabric ¼″ above top edge of binding. Press. With red thread, stitch through folded fabric all around skirt just above binding. Press fold flat over binding.

For bodice, cut 4 pieces from red miniprint, following dimensions given in Diagram 1. With right sides facing, sew left bodice front to left bodice back along shoulder seams. Repeat for remaining bodice pieces. Gather sleeve cuffs and

inner bodice edges as indicated in Diagram 1.

To finish inner edges of bodice, cut 2 (5½″ x 2″) strips from red miniprint. With wrong sides facing, press 1 strip in half lengthwise. Baste long raw edges together. With right sides facing and raw edges aligned, pin gathered edge of 1 bodice front/back to long edge of 1 strip; gather bodice to fit. Stitch. Press seam allowance toward sleeve. Repeat with second strip and bodice half.

Cut 2 (4″) lengths of double-bound eyelet trim. Gather sleeve to fit trim. Sandwich raw edge of sleeve between the 2 layers of binding and pin. Stitch with white thread. Repeat with other sleeve.

Slipstitch bodice fronts together from bottom edges up to X. (See Diagram 1.) With right sides facing, pin bodice front to back and stitch both underarm and side seams. Clip underarm angle and turn.

Mark skirt into quarters with pins. Gather skirt top. With right sides facing, match center front of skirt to center front of bodice, side pins with side seams, and center back with bodice back opening. Draw up gathers and adjust evenly. Stitch skirt to bodice.

Cut a 2″ length of pleated eyelet trim. Tack it to wrong side of bodice front so that ruffle shows at neck. (See Diagram 2.) Sew a small snap to back of dress just above waist.

To make apron skirt, cut a 4½″ x 24″ rectangle from white fabric. With compass, draw an

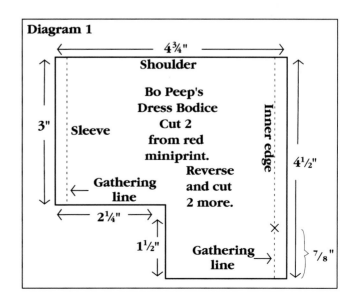

Diagram 1

4¾″

Shoulder

Bo Peep's
Dress Bodice
Cut 2
from red
miniprint.
Reverse
and cut
2 more.

3″

Sleeve

Inner edge

4½″

Gathering line

2¼″

1½″

Gathering line

⅞″

arc at each corner of apron, as in Diagram 3. Trim fabric along arcs. Cut a 29″ length of double-bound eyelet trim. Sandwich the bottom and curved edges of the apron between the 2 layers of binding, pin, and stitch. Trim excess eyelet.

Cut a 29″ length of flat lace. Stitch lace along binding just above eyelet. With pins, mark top of apron skirt into quarters. Gather top of apron skirt ¼″ from edge.

To make waistband and tie, cut a 1¾″ x 22″ strip from white fabric. With right sides facing, fold strip in half lengthwise and stitch along long edge, leaving ends open. Turn and press, with seam at bottom. Tuck ends in ¼″ and press.

Gather top of apron skirt to measure 8″. Matching center of skirt to center of waistband, pin waistband to right side of apron skirt over gathers, allowing excess to extend beyond skirt for ties. Topstitch waistband to apron skirt.

To make apron shoulder straps, cut 2 (4½″) lengths of double-bound eyelet trim. Pin 1 length to inside waistband, with 1 end 1″ from center front of apron skirt and other end at edge of skirt in back. (Eyelet edge should face arm.) Repeat for other shoulder strap. To make apron bib, pin a 2″ strip of pleated eyelet trim between shoulder straps to wrong side of apron front so that waistband just hides binding and ruffle points up.

Topstitch along top of apron waistband to secure shoulder straps and eyelet bib inset.

Continue topstitching along all edges of waist ties. Topstitch inner edge of shoulder straps, securing the 2 layers of binding and catching edges of the eyelet bib inset. With lacy edge toward top of apron, sew 8″ of flat lace on right side of waistband.

To make hat, cut a 4″ x 6″ rectangle from white fabric. With right sides facing, fold fabric in half lengthwise. Sew ends together. Clip corners, turn, and press. Press under ¼″ along raw edges. Sew binding edge of pleated eyelet trim to wrong side of hat around edges. Sew buttons just inside upper corners on front and back of hat.

To make petticoat, cut an 8″ x 24″ rectangle from white fabric. Narrowly hem 1 long edge. Pin 24″ of pleated eyelet along wrong side of hem so that binding is hidden. Sew in place. With right sides facing, fold fabric in half widthwise. Sew ends together for center back seam.

To make waist casing, press ¼″ on top raw edge of petticoat to wrong side. Fold over ¼″ again and press. Sew close to bottom fold, leaving 1″ opening. Tie 6″ of elastic to a tiny safety pin and thread elastic through casing. Remove safety pin and stitch elastic ends together. Trim excess. Sew casing opening closed.

To make pantalets, cut 4 pieces of white fabric, following dimensions given in Diagram 4. With right sides of 2 pieces facing, sew side seam. Repeat with other 2 pieces. With right sides facing, sew front pieces together along center seam. Repeat for back pieces.

Make waist casing and thread elastic as for petticoat above. With right sides facing, sew

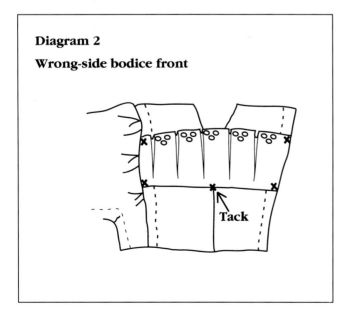

Diagram 2

Wrong-side bodice front

Tack

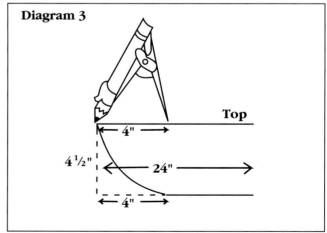

Diagram 3

Top

4″

4½″   24″

4″

front to back along inseam. Clip curves and turn. Narrowly hem legs.

To make staff, cut a 16½″ length from hanger using wire cutters. With pliers, bend wire to shape staff as in photograph. Wrap staff with 1″-wide strips of newspaper. Tape strips to secure to hanger. Continue until staff is approximately ¼″ thick. Cover newspaper with brown florists' tape, overlapping edges and stretching tape slightly as you wrap. Tape holly to front of staff, 1½″ below top of crook. Tie a multi-looped ribbon bow just below holly.

Sheep

Materials for 1 sheep:
pattern on page 139
tracing paper
17″ x 19″ piece of white fabric
long needle
1 skein white fingering-weight yarn
2 (⅛″) black shank buttons
⅔ yard (¼″-wide) red ribbon
1 (¾″) jingle bell
water-soluble marker

Note: All seams are ¼″ unless otherwise noted.

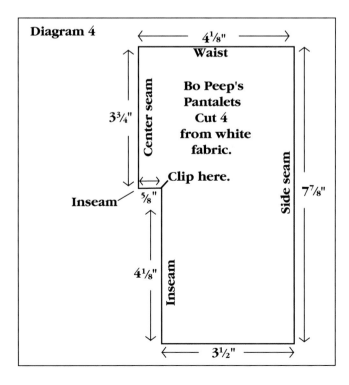

Diagram 4

4⅛″
Waist

Center seam

3¾″

Bo Peep's
Pantalets
Cut 4
from white
fabric.

Clip here.

Inseam   ⅝″

Side seam

7⅞″

Inseam

4⅛″

3½″

Transfer patterns to tracing paper. Pin pattern pieces to fabric and cut out as indicated. Transfer all pattern markings to fabrics with the water-soluble marker.

To make sheep, fold ear piece along fold line, with right sides facing, and sew, leaving opening as indicated on pattern piece. Clip curves, turn, and press. Turn under ¼″ on raw edge and slip-stitch opening closed. Repeat twice more for second ear and tail.

With right sides facing, sew head gusset to both body pieces, matching dots. With right sides facing, sew body pieces together, leaving opening as indicated on pattern piece. Clip curves and turn. Firmly stuff body. Slipstitch opening closed.

With right sides facing, sew 2 leg pieces together, leaving opening as indicated on pattern. Clip curves, turn, and press. Repeat 3 times more for 4 legs. Stuff legs firmly and blindstitch openings closed. Thread a long needle with 4 strands of thread. Position front legs in place on body at Xs. Sew back and forth several times through both legs and body, pulling thread tight and ending with 3 or 4 short stitches to secure. Repeat to attach back legs. Stitch ears and tail in position as indicated on pattern.

To make yarn loops, cut 6 (1-yard) strands of yarn and lay side by side. Thread needle with white sewing thread. Loop the 6 strands over forefinger. Tack base of loop to sheep's body. (See Diagram 5.) Continue making loops and tacking to sheep along indicated rows until entire body is covered. Clip row of loops at forehead to form sheep's "bangs."

Sew button eyes in position as indicated. String bell on the ribbon and tie around the sheep's neck.

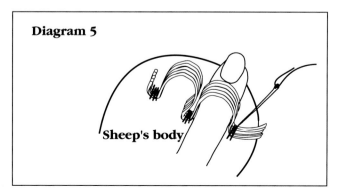

Diagram 5

Sheep's body

Greetings for The Holidays

These block-print and embossed cards look as if they had been designed in Santa's Print Shop, but you won't need the help of his elves to make them.

Use your imagination to make other Christmas shapes, such as ball ornaments, holly leaves and berries, poinsettias, or stars; design a whole array of these handsome cards. Santa's elves may very well call on you next year to make *their* Christmas cards.

Block-Print Cards

Materials:
patterns on page 129
foam-core board or smooth side of
    Styrofoam egg cartons or meat trays
graphite paper (to transfer patterns)
#2 pencil
stiff cardboard or ¼" plywood, ½" to 1"
    larger all around than pattern
sharp craft knife
white craft glue
metal ruler
white card-stock paper
dried-up ballpoint pen
acrylic paints: red, green, gold, white
4 (¼") paintbrushes
fine-point permanent black marker for
    details

For package and tree, transfer pattern to foam-core. Also transfer pattern to cardboard piece. Using craft knife in sawing motion, cut pattern pieces out of foam-core. To simulate branches on tree, score along branches with knife. Glue pattern pieces to cardboard base inside traced design. Let dry ½ hour.

For bunny design, cut 1 (3¾" x 5¾") rectangle from foam-core and glue to cardboard. Let dry ½ hour. Using craft knife and metal ruler as a guide, cut a relief of the checkerboard and heart border, leaving a 2½" x 4½" interior rectangle for bunny. Cut out bunny and holly to

form recessed portion of block. Using pencil point, punch holes for snowflake design in bunny background. Be careful to space holes evenly and to offset rows. (See photograph.)

For bunny and package designs, cut 1 (6¼" x 9") piece from card-stock paper. For tree design, cut 1 (8" x 9¼") piece from card-stock paper. Before folding cards, score along fold line, using ruler and dried-up ballpoint pen. (This will keep paper fibers from breaking along fold line.) Fold. Before applying paint to foam-core, center design in proper position on card-stock paper and indicate position with light pencil mark.

Apply paint quickly and liberally to foam-core. (It is important to work quickly at this point, since paint dries very fast.) Carefully place block on card within pencil marks and press firmly without shifting. Lift carefully. Using brush, dab paint onto any unprinted area that is important to design; however, slight irregularities add to the charm of the block print. Let dry ½ hour. With black marker, add bunny's eye; on tree, outline ornament top and add hook. Using brush, paint ornament top gold and bunny's tie and holly bow green. Using points previously made with pencil as a guide, dot snowflakes around bunny with white paint.

Reapply paint to block for each additional card. When finished, wipe excess paint off blocks with damp paper towels.

Embossed Cards

Materials:
patterns on page 133
tracing paper (to transfer patterns)
³⁄₁₆" foam-core board
sharp craft knife
plastic netting (net bags for citrus fruits)
8½" x 5½" sheets of white paper (80#
    postcard-weight)
small sponge, dampened
standard 5½" envelopes

Note: Some craft stores sell precut foam-core board shapes.

Transfer patterns onto foam-core and cut out with craft knife. Cut a piece of plastic netting measuring at least 6" x 7". Place foam-core

Left: Once the design is cut from foam-core board, a number of these Block-Print Cards can be printed in no time.

Right: *The relief design of these elegant Embossed Cards is achieved by pressing dampened postcard-weight paper over foam-core board shapes and netting.*

shape in center of netting. Fold paper in half to form 4¼" x 5½" card. Open card. With dampened sponge, lightly moisten front half of card. Place over foam-core shape and netting. Carefully finger-press dampened paper on materials, making sure not to tear the paper. Lift card and set aside to dry.

Try Stamping: It's Worth Repeating

Whether you repeat a single design or combine several, you can stamp your way to holiday fun with these projects. No matter how you try it, this repetition is never dull.

Right: A small halved pear makes a fun border design for this towel. Cut two strips of muslin. Stack strips and baste together along raw edges to make a double-layered strip. Apply acrylic paint to cut side of pear (refer to "Make Your Own Stamp Pad" below), center vertically, and stamp onto strip. Using a fabric marker, add leaf detail. Let dry. Turn under raw edges and topstitch muslin strip to purchased towel near bottom edge. Fuse decorative trim to muslin along stitching lines.

Above: There's nothing more special than greeting cards that you make yourself. Gather purchased blank cards, felt-tip markers, ink pads, and stamps of your choice. For a tree with branches so natural-looking you can almost smell the Christmassy scent, try making a tree on a card by stamping with fresh greenery spread with ink or paint. Draw candles, trunk, and base with felt-tip markers. A little glue and glitter will add sparkle to candle flames and star.

Right: It's as easy as 1-2-3 to make these colorful napkins. Just cut squares of heavy checked cotton gingham. Then staystitch one inch from edges and pull threads to fringe. Wash and iron. To prepare paint and pad, refer to "Make Your Own Stamp Pad" below. Stamp design on border checks. Let paint dry thoroughly.

Make Your Own Stamp Pad

Spread a small amount of acrylic paint on a scrap of white felt. Using a paintbrush, mix a little water with paint to thin it. Dip stamp in thinned paint. Stamp first on scrap paper to remove excess paint, and then stamp on chosen material.

Left: Combined designs on this stamped sampler create a one-of-a-kind look. Use lined notebook paper to simplify placement and centering. First, experiment with combinations of stamps on the lined paper. When you find an arrangement you like, place lined paper on top of heavy white paper precut to fit your frame. Punching through lined paper with a #2 pencil, lightly dot design lines on white paper. Use design on lined paper and pencil dots on white paper as guides to stamping your sampler.

Above: Stamp your way through myriad greetings this year. A variety of mediums lend themselves to the art of stamping. Acrylic paints work well on fabrics, and ink or felt-tip markers can be used very effectively on paper. You can purchase plastic or rubber stamps (see source listing on page 154), cut your own designs into square rubber erasers, or make stamps from natural elements, such as fruit. Just set out blank greeting cards and brown or white wrapping paper. Then let your imagination take over!

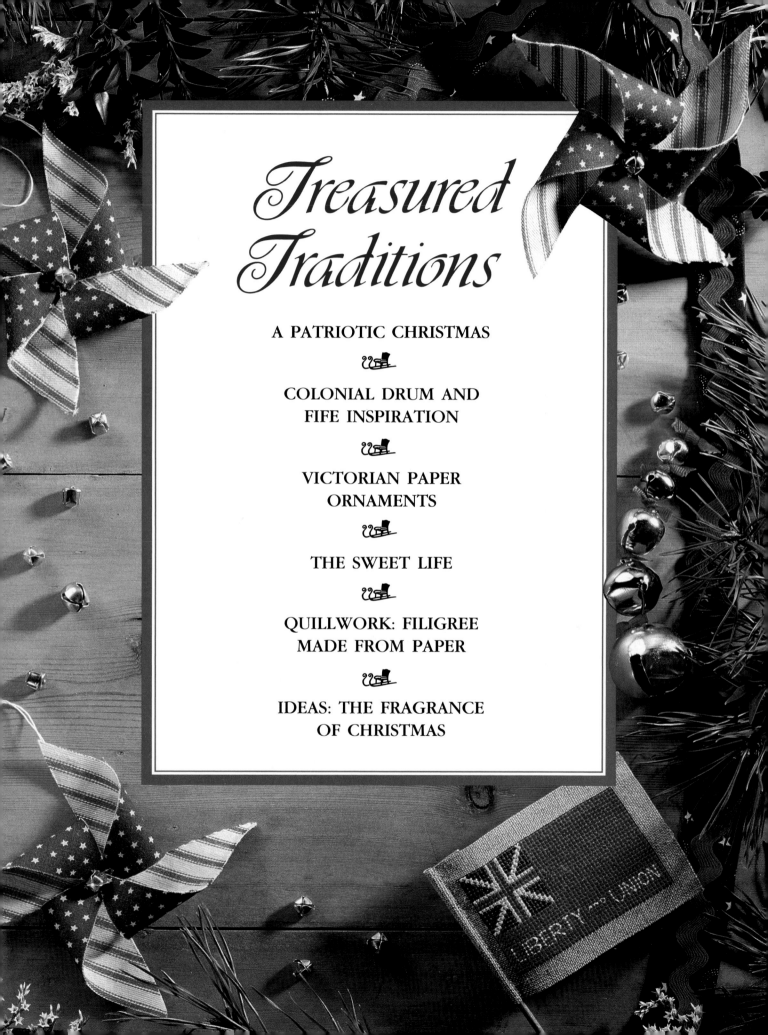

Treasured Traditions

A PATRIOTIC CHRISTMAS

COLONIAL DRUM AND
FIFE INSPIRATION

VICTORIAN PAPER
ORNAMENTS

THE SWEET LIFE

QUILLWORK: FILIGREE
MADE FROM PAPER

IDEAS: THE FRAGRANCE
OF CHRISTMAS

A Patriotic Christmas

The patriotic tree, decked in red, white, and blue ornaments, was an American innovation a century ago. Looking for ways to express their brotherhood and pride in country, people began to explore variations on the traditionally trimmed tree. Thus, the patriotic tree, which included an abundance of American flags, became quite popular in many homes.

You can re-create this American tradition for your own home with the easy-to-make projects shown here.

Fabric Pinwheels

Materials for 18 pinwheels:
¼ yard (45″-wide) red-and-white ticking
¼ yard (45″-wide) blue cotton fabric with
   small white stars
1½ yards paper-backed fusible web
thread to match
18 (⅝″) gold jingle bells
4 yards (⅛″-wide) red satin ribbon
craft glue

Following manufacturer's instructions, fuse fabrics with wrong sides facing. Cut into 18 (4″) squares.

With striped side of fused fabrics up, mark center of 1 square. With ruler and pencil, lightly draw a line between corners, forming an X. With scissors, cut along each marked line to within ½″ of center.

With striped side up, fold every other point to center, overlapping center mark slightly. (See photograph on page 59.) Tack points to center of pinwheel. Tack 1 bell to center.

For hanger, cut 1 (8″) piece of ribbon and knot loose ends together. Glue ribbon to back of 1 outer point of pinwheel.

Repeat for remaining pinwheels.

Below: Ribbon festoons on the tree and mantel, old-fashioned toys, and packages wrapped in red, white, and blue carry out the patriotic theme. To order eagles (on package) and Dresden stars (gold sunbursts on tree), see source listing on page 154.

Stuffed Horse Ornament

Materials for 1 ornament:
pattern on page 144
¼ yard (45″-wide) striped fabric
tan household dye
cardboard or plastic template material
tracing paper
#2 pencil
matching thread
polyester stuffing
dowel or large knitting needle for stuffing
   tool
cotton sock to match fabric
matching embroidery floss
black embroidery floss for eyes
embroidery needle
scrap of wool fabric for blanket
2 (½″) self-adhesive gold paper stars

Note: All seam allowances are ¼″.

Wash fabric to remove sizing. To give fabric an aged look, following manufacturer's instructions, dye fabric in a solution of ½ teaspoon dye to 1 gallon water. Allow to dry. Press.

Trace pattern pieces onto template material and cut out templates. Transfer pattern shapes and markings to fabric. Cut out.

With right sides facing and raw edges aligned, stitch gusset pieces together across top between dots. With right sides facing and raw edges aligned, stitch 2 body pieces together across top between dots, leaving an opening as indicated.

With right sides facing and matching dots and seam lines, pin body to gusset. Stitch.

Clip seam allowance almost to stitching line along curves and at sharp corners. Turn. Using dowel for hard-to-reach places, stuff horse firmly. Whipstitch opening closed.

To make tail, cut 1 (4″) section from top of cotton sock and unravel yarn. Make a bundle of 6″ strands of raveled yarn and tie together in middle. Tack knot to horse as indicated by T on pattern. Trim and fluff strands as desired.

To make mane, in same manner, tie and tack small bundles of raveled yarn along horse's head and neck between M marks. Trim and fluff.

To make hooves, leaving a 2″ tail of floss at beginning and end, tightly wrap 1 (8″) strand of matching embroidery floss about ½″ from bottom of 1 leg. Knot thread to secure. Thread ends in needle; run ends into leg and trim to

conceal ends. Repeat to make 3 more hooves.

Make eyes with French knots and 2 strands of black embroidery floss.

Tack blanket to horse's back. Stick 1 gold star on each side of blanket. Using needle and thread, make a hanger by stitching a thread loop to horse's back.

Paper Hat Ornament

Materials for 1 ornament:
pattern on page 144
damp sponge
red acrylic paint
scrap of plain white paper
tracing paper
photocopy of all-text page from children's
   book (or other large-print text)

Dip damp sponge in a few drops of paint on paper plate. Dab paint on 1 side of plain white paper. Set aside to dry.

From photocopied paper, cut 1 (5½″ x 7¾″) rectangle. With plain sides facing, fold paper in half to measure 3⅞″ x 5½″. (See Diagram 1.) To make hat crown, turn each corner of folded side down to make triangles, meeting at center and stopping 1¼″ from bottom. (See Diagram 2.) To make hat brim, fold bottom edges up over sides of hat.

Trace feather pattern onto painted paper and cut out. With scissors, cut slits all around, leaving center of feather uncut.

To make holder for feather, cut 2 (¼″) parallel slits in brim of hat.

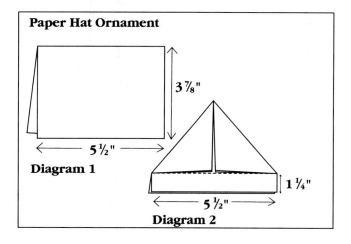

Paper Hat Ornament

3⅞″

5½″

Diagram 1

1¼″

5½″

Diagram 2

Jingle Bell Ornament

Materials for 1 ornament:
12″ (26-gauge) gold spool bead wire
1 (35-mm) gold jingle bell
1 (25-mm) silver jingle bell
1 (20-mm) gold jingle bell
1 (16-mm) silver jingle bell
1 (13-mm) gold jingle bell
12½″ (¼″-wide) red grosgrain ribbon

Insert 1 end of wire through top loop of 35-mm gold bell. Twist short end of wire several times around top loop of bell to secure. Thread other end of wire through bottom of 25-mm silver bell. Pull end of wire through top loop of smaller bell, pushing smaller bell close to larger bell. Loop wire through smaller bell's top loop and pull wire tight to secure, keeping bells in alignment.

Repeat with remaining bells, using progressively smaller bells.

To make hanger, form small loop with end of wire approximately ½″ from top of smallest bell. Wrap remaining wire tightly down ½″ length of wire between loop and top of smallest bell. Cut excess wire.

Cut 5 (2½″) lengths from red ribbon. Knot 1 length of ribbon between each 2 bells and above the smallest bell at top of ornament. Trim ribbon ends.

Stars-and-Stripes Ornaments

Materials for 1 ornament:
placement diagram on page 145
purchased wooden heart or house
   ornament
fine sandpaper
clear varnish
small paintbrush
⅜″-wide masking tape
½″ self-adhesive paper stars
acrylic paints: blue, red
water-base satin varnish
9″ of twine for hanger
hot-glue gun and glue sticks

Using fine sandpaper, sand the wooden ornament until smooth. Using a small paintbrush,

seal ornament with clear varnish. Let dry.

Following diagram, block off area for stars with masking tape and place stars, pressing firmly. Using small paintbrush and painting over stars, paint area with blue acrylic paint. Let dry. Remove tape and stars.

Following diagram, use masking tape to space stripes. (On house, leave ¾″ gap in tape for doorway.) Using small paintbrush, paint area with red acrylic paint. Let dry. Remove tape.

Seal with water-base satin varnish. Let dry.

For hanger, make a loop from twine and hot-glue ends to back of ornament.

Cross-Stitched Flags

Materials for 1 flag:
chart and color key on page 145
5¾″ x 8″ piece light brown 26-count linen
embroidery floss (see color key)
embroidery needle
8″ (⅛″-diameter) dowel
gold paint
small paintbrush

Using 2 strands floss over 2 threads and beginning at center of design, center and work design on linen according to chart.

Using mild soap, wash completed piece carefully in cold water. Rinse thoroughly. Roll piece in a terry-cloth towel to remove excess water. Place stitched side down on a dry terry-cloth towel. Press. (Do not use steam.)

Leaving 1¼″ of unstitched linen on left side to fold around dowel, trim design fabric to 2¾″ x 5″. (When dowel flagpole has been added, fabric border of flag should be ½″.) For fringed border, with right side up, carefully pull 2 or 3 strands each from top, right, and bottom edges.

Paint dowel gold. Let dry.

With top edge of flag at end of dowel, fold the 1¼″ of unstitched linen around dowel. Using zipper foot, machine-stitch close to dowel to hold flag in place.

Opposite: These ornaments require so few steps that in no time you'll have enough to decorate your own patriotic tree. Clockwise, from top: Stars-and-Stripes wooden houses and heart, Cross-Stitched Flags, Fabric Pinwheels, and Stuffed Horses.

Treetop Santa

Materials:
chart and color key on page 147
5" square of ivory 14-count Aida
5" square of muslin
embroidery floss (see color key)
embroidery needle
polyester stuffing
11" x 17" piece of medium-weight cardboard
hot-glue gun and glue sticks
½ yard red woven wool flannel
¼ yard white polar fleece or flannel
scrap of coordinating fabric
1 tiny ribbon bow and 2 gold bells for neck
   trim
24" of small decorative cord
6" x 8" piece of burlap
18" (⅛"-wide) red-and-green striped
   grosgrain ribbon
cinnamon sticks, miniature toys, ornaments,
   artificial greenery, and berries for Santa's
   pack

Left: This Treetop Santa, dressed in woven wool flannel, carries a burlap pack filled with treats for good little girls and boys. The secret to finishing this old-fashioned Santa quickly is folding and gluing the coat and hood, instead of sewing.

Tea Dyeing

It takes very little time to give plain fabrics an old-fashioned appearance. Ordinary household dyes work well to give your handcrafted projects an antique look, but plain old tea can work for you, too.

When tea-dyeing, you'll get the best results from fabrics of 100-percent cotton or other natural fibers. Cotton and polyester blends will dye, but they will take a bit longer to absorb the color. It's best to stay away from synthetics such as nylon or Orlon.

A few easy steps will give your fabric a timeworn look. Use a half-gallon of very hot tap water to 16 tea bags and allow to steep about 20 minutes. Remove bags and stir well.

Dip your fabric into the tea and let it soak, checking every 5 minutes for depth of color. It takes between 10 and 35 minutes to achieve an aged effect. *Note:* Fabric, when dry, will be lighter than it appears when wet.

When your fabric seems just a little darker than you want it to be, remove it from the tea and squeeze. If the stain seems too dark, rinse with water. Place the fabric in a clothes dryer with an old terry-cloth towel to absorb tea residue. When thoroughly dry, press with warm iron to set the color.

For face and head, cross-stitch design on Aida, following chart. With design centered, trim design piece to 2¾" x 4½". Trim muslin to match. With right sides facing and using ¼" seam, stitch around face, rounding top of head and leaving bottom open for stuffing. Turn and stuff. Set aside.

For base, roll cardboard into cone shape with 4¼" bottom diameter. Glue sides together. Trim bottom even so that cone will stand straight. Leaving 1½" opening at top, trim top so that finished cone is 8½" tall. Set aside.

For coat, cut 1 (15½" x 19") piece from wool flannel. For coat collar, fold 1 long side over 1" and press. Fold over another 1½" and pin. For hem, repeat along other long edge.

To wrap coat around cardboard base, place coat on flat surface, folded sides down. Center cone on coat with hem and bottom of cone aligned. Adjusting folds and pinning as needed, wrap coat around cone. (See photograph.) Fold collar ends all the way down to hem to form front facing. Tuck ends of collar inside upper fold of hem and glue. Glue hem in place around coat. Glue bottom of coat around cone. Cut 1 (1" x 18") strip from fleece and glue around coat hem.

For hood, cut 1 (7½" x 11½") piece from wool flannel. For hood facing, fold 1 long edge over 1" and then 1" again. Press fold and glue in place. Insert head into cone opening. Wrap hood fabric around head and insert bottom edges inside coat neckline.

For sleeves, cut 2 (5¼" x 6") pieces from wool flannel. For sleeve cuff, on 5¼" edge of 1 sleeve piece, fold over ¾" and then 1" again. Press cuff and glue in place. For arm, place a 2½"-long roll of polyester stuffing lengthwise along center on wrong side of sleeve piece. Roll sleeve over stuffing to form a tube. Glue seam closed. Cut 1 (1" x 5¾") strip from fleece and glue in place around cuff. With seam toward body, slip stuffed sleeve under edge of collar and glue in place. Repeat for second sleeve.

Glue scrap of coordinating fabric to top of cone at neckline to cover cardboard. Add bow and bells to center of neck for trim. Knot ends of decorative cord and tie around waist.

For pack, fold burlap in half widthwise to measure 4" x 6". With right sides facing and using ¼" seam, stitch around 3 sides. Turn. Pull threads to make ¼" fringe along open edge.

Turn down fringed edge 1¼". Stuff pack ¾ full with polyester stuffing. Wrap grosgrain ribbon around pack under fringed fold and bring around shoulders. Knot ribbon ends at bottom front of hood and tuck ends inside coat to conceal. Glue center of pack to back of coat to anchor securely.

Fill remainder of pack with cinnamon sticks, miniature toys, ornaments, artificial greenery, and berries.

Patriotic Tree Skirt

Materials:
pattern on page 143
3 yards (45"-wide) red miniprint fabric for lining
5½ yards (45"-wide) red-and-white ticking for skirt top, piping, ties, and bias strip for center circle
½ yard (45"-wide) navy star-print fabric for tassel appliqué
½ yard (45"-wide) red star-print fabric for swag appliqué
tan household dye
several sheets of tissue or wrapping paper
#2 pencil
30" of string
pushpin or thumbtack
tracing paper
2½ yards paper-backed fusible web
7 yards (¼"-diameter) cording for piping

To give fabrics an aged appearance, following manufacturer's instructions, dye fabrics in a solution of 1 teaspoon dye to each gallon water. (Or follow directions for dyeing with tea on page 64.) Dry and press all fabrics.

To make pattern, tape several sheets of tissue paper together to make 1 (60") square. Mark center of square with a pencil dot. Fold square in half and then into fourths. Now fold on diagonal, with folded edges together.

To make circle, attach string to tissue at dot with pushpin. Measure 27" of string and tie remaining string to pencil to make a compass. Holding string taut, draw an arc with a 27" radius on the folded tissue. To make center circle, draw an arc with a 2½″ radius in the same manner. (See Diagram on page 38.) Cut out both circles along marked lines. Unfold tissue. Using fold lines as guide, cut circle in half. Use 1 half as pattern for lining. From remaining half, cut away 1 panel to make pattern for skirt top panels. Discard remaining 3 tissue panels.

For lining, align straight edges of lining pattern with grain line of miniprint fabric and pin to fabric. Adding ½″ seam allowance, cut out to make half of lining. Repeat for other half of lining. Set lining pieces aside.

Fold skirt top panel pattern in half lengthwise to determine grain line and mark with arrow. Unfold pattern. For skirt top, adding ½″ seam allowance, cut 8 panels from ticking. *Note:* When cutting, place pattern to make sure that stripes will match when sewn. Set panels aside.

Above: Use tan household dye to give an antique appearance to the tree skirt; fuse swags and tassels to ticking to complete the patriotic motif. String silver and gold bells in graduated sizes to make the jingle bell ornament. "Stick a feather" in the folded paper hat for an ornament finished in a jiffy.

From remaining ticking, cut 1¼″-wide bias strips, piecing as needed to equal 9½ yards. From this, cut 1 (7-yard) length. Make 7 yards corded piping. Set piping and remaining bias strips aside.

Make pattern for swag and tassel appliqués. (Do not add seam allowance.) Following manufacturer's instructions, fuse web to wrong side of red star-print fabric and navy star-print fabric. Trace and cut 8 swags from red fabric and 7 tassels from navy fabric. Peel off paper backing and discard.

To make skirt top, with right sides facing and stripes matching, stitch 2 panels together along long edges. Continue joining panels, leaving first and last panels unjoined. Press all seams open.

To fuse appliqués to skirt top, centering tassel on seam, place tassel 2½″ from bottom of skirt. Pin in place. With tips of swag appliqué overlapping tassel as indicated on pattern and center scallop 2″ from bottom of skirt, arrange appliqués on 1 ticking panel. (See photograph.) Pin in place. Repeat with remaining appliqués. Following manufacturer's instructions, fuse appliqués to skirt.

With right sides facing and raw edges aligned, pin piping down 1 straight edge, around bottom of skirt, and up opposite straight edge. Using zipper foot, stitch piping to skirt, stitching on stitching line of piping.

To make lining, with right sides facing and raw edges aligned, stitch together lining pieces along 1 long edge. With right sides facing and raw edges aligned, pin lining to skirt top. Leaving center circle open for turning, stitch lining to skirt top along sides and bottom, stitching on stitching line of piping. Trim seam allowances, clip curves, and turn.

To bind center circle, cut 1 (48½″) length from bias strip. With right sides facing and raw edges aligned, pin bias strip around center circle so that a 14″ tail extends beyond each side for ties. Stitch bias strip to skirt. Fold strip to back of skirt, turn under ¼″ seam allowance on raw edges, and slipstitch to lining. Topstitch ties close to all edges.

For middle ties, cut 2 (14″) pieces from remaining bias strip. Fold under ¼″ on each long edge and press. Fold under each end ¼″. Fold ties in half lengthwise, wrong sides facing. Topstitch close to all edges. Stitch 1 tie to lining at midpoint on each straight edge of skirt opening.

Colonial Drum And Fife Inspiration

George Washington crossed the Delaware River one freezing Christmas night to win his first great victory of the American Revolution—over Hessian troops at Trenton. In the camp as he left, there was music urging his soldiers along. The fife, a woodwind instrument in the flute family, has been synonymous with colonial American history ever since that time.

Fife and drum corps throughout the country perpetuate and preserve colonial, military, and traditional forms of American field music. The Colonial Drum and Fife Corps of Alton, Illinois, has cheered presidents Ford, Carter, and Reagan. This corps is one of only two in the nation allowed to perform at Colonial Williamsburg in Virginia. When the corps was formed in 1975 by Dr. Harvey Veit, it boasted only one fifer and one drummer, much like the original field musicians of the American Revolution. Today the Alton corps has 35 musicians, ranging in age from 10 to 18 years.

When the corps performs for Christmas parades, the crowds hear fifers fifing, the steady rhythm of drums, and flags flapping in the freezing winter breeze. Young hearts continue to be inspired by the challenge of this tradition.

The Colonial Drum and Fife Corps travels as many as 7,000 miles a year for up to 60 performances in Canada, Indiana, Missouri, and Illinois. The photos on this page show the corps braving subfreezing temperatures for the Christian Hills Christmas Homes Tour in Alton, Illinois.

Early Settlers' Christmas

A biting wind hits their faces as the horse draws the carriage through moonlit snow to evening church services. It's late, but the children's eyes shine like stars. In the distance they see a small, white wooden church. A candle glows in each window. A cedar wreath hangs on the door. Inside, other worshippers and

Left: St. Peter's Church, the first Catholic church in Milwaukee, was built in 1839, but has been renovated to reflect its 1889 appearance, a fusion of Greek Revival and Gothic architectural traditions.

neighbors sing hymns and warm themselves by the heat of a black potbellied stove. All hearts sing praise to the newborn Babe, but all eyes drink up another wondrous sight.

By the altar stands a giant cedar tree adorned with popcorn garlands and tiny shimmering candles. Nestled in the boughs are hand-sewn rag dolls, wooden spinning tops, a tatting shuttle, small cornucopias filled with candies, and a rare treat—oranges.

It's Christmas Eve in the 1880s. These midwesterners know that they'll receive a gift this night, chosen from this Christmas tree. For many, this is the first glimpse of a decorated tree, since it is not yet the tradition to have a tree in the home.

In Old World Wisconsin on a cold December afternoon over a century later, school children bundled in mittens and mufflers huddle again around a black potbellied stove, singing Christmas carols.

Set in the hills of the Kettle Moraine State Forest, Old World Wisconsin is a village museum that has preserved the state's architectural and cultural heritage. Historic structures, nestled into the 576-acre site, include a town hall, farmhouses, barns, stables—50 buildings in all—built by Wisconsin pioneers in the 19th and early 20th centuries.

Owned and operated by the State Historical Society of Wisconsin, Old World Wisconsin portrays the diverse ethnic heritage of a state that includes people with German, Polish, Finnish, Norwegian, and Danish ancestry. Visitors experience 19th-century rural Wisconsin, brought to life by authentically costumed interpreters.

School children restless with Christmas anticipation can visit the museum for a field day excursion and leave with a memory of a simple Christmas long ago when their ancestors rode in carriages instead of cars.

Opposite: Bible quotations were the inspiration for certain church decorations. Wire shaped into large letters was wrapped with greenery. Sometimes simple phrases were used. Other times entire verses from the Bible could be seen covering the walls.

Above: Dressed in costumes of the period, these ladies portray life in the 1880s. Heat radiates from the stove in the center of the church to warm all corners.

Left: These china dolls resting in an antique carriage represent the kind of gifts that would have been presented around the church Christmas tree.

Victorian Paper Ornaments

The idea of making a treasure from a few bits of scrap paper was just as intriguing to the ladies of the 19th century as it is to us today.

Paper dolls and cotton batting ornaments are two of the styles of Christmas decorations that were prevalent at the turn of the century. Bring your whole family together in renewing this old-time craft.

Pink Paper Doll

Materials:
pattern and diagram on page 146
9″ jointed paper doll or 11″ regular paper doll
2 brass brads for jointed doll or 4 brass brads for regular doll
crepe paper: pink, green (1 package each)
rubber cement
pink thread
crepe paper roses
cotton balls (optional)
miniature straw basket
white glue

Above: Paper dolls were in demand as toys in the 1800s, but they were not popular as tree ornaments until the turn of the century.

Note: For information about ordering paper dolls, see source listing on page 154.

If using a jointed paper doll, assemble the body and legs. Set arms aside. If using a regular paper doll, cut the legs off at the thighs and re-attach with brads, being careful to make doll 9" tall when attached. Cut off the arms at the shoulders and set aside.

To make bodice, cut 1 (3" x 10") rectangle from pink crepe paper. Turn under ½" hem along each long edge. Using your fingers, gather bodice around upper torso, covering chest and back, and attach to doll with rubber cement.

To make ruffled skirt, cut 4 (4" x 18") strips from pink crepe paper with grain running width-wise. Fold each in half lengthwise. For each strip, run a row of gathering stitches ¼" from long raw edges through both layers. Set 1 strip aside. Gather each of 3 remaining strips to 9" and take 2 or 3 stitches to secure.

To make underskirt, cut 1 (9" x 4") rectangle from pink crepe paper with grain running from top to bottom. Baste top gathered edge of first ruffle 1" from bottom 9" edge of underskirt. Baste top of second ruffle 2" from bottom edge, and top of third ruffle 3" from bottom edge. (See Diagram on page 146.)

Run a row of gathering stitches ¼" from top edge of underskirt. Gather to fit waist. Gather remaining ruffle that was set aside to fit waist

and baste to top edge of underskirt. Glue skirt in place on doll with rubber cement.

To make sash, cut 1 (1½" x 12") strip from green crepe paper, with grain running length-wise. Fold both long edges in ½" to form ½" x 12" strip. Wrap sash around waist tightly, cover-ing edges of skirt and bodice. Glue in place with rubber cement. Tie a crepe paper bow. Trim sash with bow and roses. (See photograph.)

For sleeves, transfer pattern onto pink crepe paper, being careful to observe the grain. Run a row of gathering stitches along each sleeve at curved edge as indicated on pattern. Turn up hem and stitch. Run a row of gathering stitches above hem as indicated. Attach a brad to top of each arm. Slip arm into sleeve so that top of arm is covered. (Cotton balls may be stuffed in the top of sleeve to make it puff.) Pull gathering threads to fit top and bottom of sleeve around arm. Secure threads. Cut a strip of green crepe paper, wrap around gathering stitches at cuff, and tie in bow. Repeat for other sleeve.

Glue basket to hand with white glue. Position the arms naturally at the shoulders and re-attach with brads.

Make and glue small green crepe paper bows on shoes and hair.

Opposite: Create a parade of Victorian paper dolls to decorate your mantel. These dolls were borrowed from the collection of Nada Gray, author of Holidays: Victorian Women Celebrate in Pennsylvania. *For information about how to order a copy, see source listing on page 154.*

Doll Up the Holidays

In the 19th century, when little girls were taught fine hand sew-ing, they practiced these skills while making clothes for their paper dolls. They would raid their mothers' sewing boxes for scraps of lace to trim the "real" dresses.

Perhaps their moth-ers longed to play, too, for by the early 1900s, paper dolls dressed in velvets and laces began to be used in home deco-rating. Eventually, paper dolls were seen during the holidays even on the tree.

Above: Also referred to as cotton-wadding, cotton-wool, and pressed-cotton ornaments, these doll-like figures were often kept out as playthings long after other decorations were packed away.

Cotton Batting Girl and Santa

Materials for girl:
pattern on page 144
posterboard
scrap picture of girl's face, 1″ in diameter
white glue
black acrylic paint
paintbrush
1 white pipe cleaner
7″ x 9″ piece of white cotton batting
4″ x 9″ piece of pink tissue paper
small lacquered holly leaf
6¼″ (¼″-wide) pink satin ribbon

Note: For information about ordering reproduction scrap pictures, see source listing on page 154.

Transfer pattern to posterboard and cut out. Glue scrap face to top of girl form. Paint legs and shoes black.

For arms, cut 1 (7″) length of pipe cleaner and fold in each end ½″. Cut 1 (3″ x 7″) rectangle of batting. Lay pipe cleaner lengthwise along center of batting. Fold batting ends over folded pipe cleaner ends and glue in place. Roll batting loosely around pipe cleaner and glue in place.

Lightly spread glue on body front and back at knee area. For skirt, fold tissue paper lengthwise and pleat (with fold at bottom) around figure, starting from back and keeping fold of skirt just above shoe tops.

For coat, cut 1 (3¾″ x 4¾″) rectangle of batting. Spread glue on body top, front, and back. Center figure lengthwise on coat rectangle and fold batting around figure, gathering batting around neck. Lightly glue overlapped front edges of coat in place.

For hat, cut 1 (2″ x 3″) piece of batting. Fold up ½″ along 1 long edge. Glue batting piece around face. Gather at back of head and glue in place.

For collar, cut 1 (1″ x 4″) piece of batting. Fold in half lengthwise and glue collar around neck. Fit snugly, covering raw edges of coat and hat and tucking in around neck.

Center and glue arm piece around back of coat, with seam facing in. Fold arms around to front.

For muff, cut 1 (2″ x 3″) piece of batting. Fold long edges in ½″. Wrap batting piece around hands and glue with seam toward body. Tuck holly leaf in the crook of arm and glue in place. Tie small ribbon bow and glue under chin. Trim ends. Tuck small piece of ribbon in brim of hat.

Materials for Santa:
pattern on page 144
posterboard
scrap picture of Santa's face, 1″ in diameter
white glue
black acrylic paint
paintbrush
1 white pipe cleaner
7″ x 8″ piece of white cotton batting
6″ piece of red cord
3 silver beads
gold metallic pipe cleaner
sprig of preserved evergreen
small twigs tied in a bundle with thread

Referring to instructions for girl, construct Santa the same except cut 1 (4¾″ x 5¾″) rectangle of batting for his coat.

To finish Santa, thread cord with beads and tie around waist. Make buttons from snip of metallic pipe cleaner twisted into circle. Glue buttons to front of coat. Tuck piece of evergreen in 1 arm and twigs in other and glue in place.

The Sweet Life

For some children, working after school in their fathers' offices might be drudgery. But when Tom Beerntsen was a boy, his worst punishment was to be kept away. Tom's dad, Richard, owned a candy store—not one with just a few sweets here and there, but a family candy shop where candy canes, ribbon swirls, and hand-dipped chocolates were born. Tom helped in any way he was needed, learning the proper proportions of ingredients and the just-right moment when the sugar syrup was done.

Despite his love of candy making, Tom, the young man, decided to explore a career outside the candy business. He left his hometown of Manitowoc, Wisconsin, for an administrative job with the YMCA in Austin, Minnesota. But sometimes temptation is too sweet to refuse. In 1983, when Tom's father decided to retire and sell the Beerntsens' candy business, Tom came home.

Tom remembers: "I talked it over with my wife, Penny, and we decided that we just couldn't let the family business go."

"The happiest day of my life was the day Tom decided to take over the business," Richard said. "I never thought it would happen."

Beerntsen's Candies in Mantiowoc was founded in 1932 by Richard's father, Joseph. Before he settled in Manitowoc, Joe had made candy in Chicago and Milwaukee. In Chicago, he had worked with the Brach and Bunte candy companies prior to buying his own store, called The Sweet Shop. In 1922 he moved to Milwaukee and opened Joe Beerntsen's Candies.

After 10 years in Milwaukee, Joe moved to Manitowoc and opened Beerntsen's Candies at its present location. He built the shop to reflect the charm of the period, with rows of black walnut booths, mirrored shelves, archways, and chandeliers. He operated this store until his retirement in 1958, when he sold the business to his son, Richard. And Richard and his wife, Ione, operated the store for 25 years, preserving the old-fashioned atmosphere, until Tom and Penny returned to continue the sweet life—the Beerntsen candy tradition.

Right: Just add 22 pounds of sugar and a few pounds of corn syrup, heat it all in a 63-year-old copper pot, and you, too, can start a batch of 400 candy canes.

Above: Richard Beerntsen, left, followed his father into the candy business. Now his daughter-in-law Penny and son Tom continue the tradition. Will the next generation follow in the family footsteps? Penny and Tom say they'll let their children decide.

The Story of the Candy Cane

Three centuries ago the idea for a candy cane was born when a white sugar stick was used to quiet a crying baby. A pretty plain start—no stripes, no crooks, just soothing sweetness. Then in 1670 a desperate choirmaster in Cologne, Germany, held his young carolers' attention with the promise of white sugar sticks that were curved at the end to resemble shepherds' crooks.

From Cologne, candy canes spread throughout Europe, where Nativity plays were always accompanied by gifts of candy crooks.

The candy cane made its way into American holidays in the 1850s when a German-Swedish immigrant adorned a spruce tree with white candy canes. The turn of the century brought red stripes to the plain cane as peppermint was added for flavor.

Above: Although candy making can be a scientific business with exacting measurements and cooking times, Tom says he just pulls the heavy mass until he gets tired. Pulling the candy puts air into the mass and lightens the batch. As the batch is pulled and it begins to cool, the sugar tries to convert back into granules, giving the candy its whiteness.

Commercially made candy canes, mixed by machine, are filled with lots of air bubbles and are sold by the box. Beerntsen's heavy candy canes are sold by the cane and have very few bubbles.

Right: Small portions of the candy are colored with red and green vegetable dyes to make the telltale candy cane stripes.

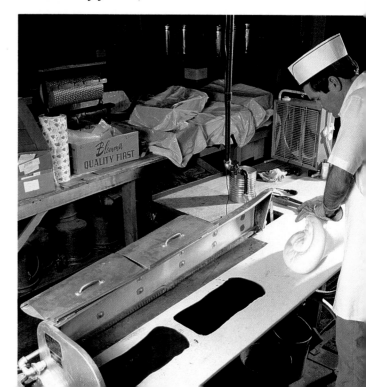

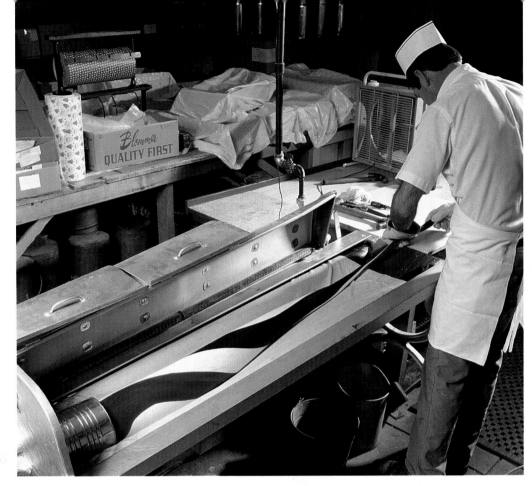

Left: As the three-layered candy block turns on the canvas mat, swirls develop. Tom once made a life-size edible baseball bat for his son to give as a gift to a schoolmate.

Below: Beerntsen's Candies makes 25,000 candy canes a year—one at a time.

Above: As the candy is swirled, the end tapers to a slim stick. Tom snips lengths of warm striped canes, while Penny shapes the crooks.

Quillwork: Filigree Made from Paper

Quillwork is the art of making tiny paper rolls and scrolls, based on either tight or loose circles. These rolls and scrolls, when glued together, make a design so intricate-looking it will seem as if it took hours and hours to complete. On the contrary, quillwork is not "skillwork"!

After you've practiced a few rolls and scrolls like those shown in the diagrams on page 153, you'll find that the craft is easily mastered. Our instructions for the delicate tree and wreath, along with the source listing on page 154, will get you started.

Materials:
pattern and diagrams on page 153
⅛″-wide white quilling paper
¹⁄₁₆″-wide white quilling paper
¹⁄₁₆″-wide red quilling paper
quilling tools, including needle tool, slotted tool, or T-pin
wax paper
4″ x 6″ piece of corrugated cardboard
craft glue
1 (2″ x 3″) and 1 (2″ x 4¼″) miniature blackboard (found at craft shops)
8″ (⅛″-wide) ivory satin ribbon

To quill, begin by measuring length of quilling paper specified in individual instructions. Tear paper rather than cut, because a torn edge will glue down more smoothly.

To quill with a needle tool or T-pin, hold tool perpendicular to work surface. With other hand, press slightly moistened end of paper strip against tool, with 1 edge of paper and point of tool resting on work surface. Wind strip around tool, *holding tool still.*

To quill with a slotted tool, thread the paper strip into slot. Slide tool almost to the end of strip and roll by *turning the tool* in a circular motion, keeping paper edges even.

Make quilling board by wrapping wax paper around corrugated cardboard. Slip pattern between wax paper and cardboard. With a straight pin, secure the first roll or scroll directly over the pattern. Place the second roll or scroll next to it. Glue sparingly where the 2 pieces touch or overlap. Continue adding rolls and scrolls, following the pattern and using pins to secure

shapes as needed. When the design is completed, let glue dry. Then gently lift the design from the wax paper, transfer to chosen background, and glue lightly in place.

Tree Ornament

Using pattern as guide, make individual marquises, teardrops, open hearts, V scrolls, C scrolls, and S scrolls from 3″ strips of ⅛″-wide white paper. Using 2″ strips of ¹⁄₁₆″-wide red paper, make loose circles for 5 tree ornaments. For the 2 square gift packages, make 4 squares each, using 3″ strips of ⅛″-wide white paper; glue squares together. For rectangular package, use same technique with 6″ strips of ⅛″-wide white paper, but form a rectangle. Make ribbons and bows from strips of ¹⁄₁₆″-wide red paper.

Lightly glue on 2″ x 4¼″ miniature blackboard. To make hanger, make a double loop with ribbon and glue to back of blackboard.

Wreath Ornament

From 3″ strips of ¹⁄₁₆″-wide white paper, make 33 teardrops. Overlapping edges, glue in circle to form wreath. (See pattern.) Using 2″ strips of ¹⁄₁₆″-wide red paper, make 5 tight circles for berries. Using 24″ strip of ¹⁄₁₆″-wide red paper, make grape roll for bell. Using 4″ strip of ¹⁄₁₆″-wide white paper, make tight circle for clapper. Glue in place. Glue wreath to 2″ x 3″ blackboard. Make hanger as for tree ornament.

Quilling Through the Centuries

Quilling probably originated in the elaborate filigree work that has been part of our art heritage since ancient times. Filigree has been found on Egyptian, Greek, and Etruscan tombs. Possibly as far back as the 13th century, a nun curled a paper strip left from trimmed Bible pages and wondered what might be done with it.

This paper copy of precious-metal filigree filled a need of the times, because members of the church felt religious symbols should be lavishly embellished. Originally, a bird feather, or quill, was used as a shaft for curling the paper.

Early settlers brought the craft from England to the American colonies, and it became very popular during the 18th century. Fine examples can be found today in museums featuring colonial exhibits.

The Fragrance of Christmas

The scent of winter spices such as allspice, cinnamon, and nutmeg wafts through our homes all during the holidays. Swags of garland and a fresh-cut Christmas tree accent the aroma. Here are a few ways to add to the fragrant essence of the season.

Christmas Tree Potpourri

When you bring the Christmas tree inside and the scents begin to rise as it warms, memories brew. You can make a lasting reminder of the holidays by snipping a few fresh green branches for Christmas potpourri.

For bulk, start with branch tips or needles from fresh-cut Fraser fir. This evergreen has a rich balsam fragrance that is long-lasting and requires no fixative. Fill your potpourri container ¾ full of fir clippings and then add your choice of the following:

For citrus-evergreen potpourri, add 2 cups fir tips, ½ cup bay leaves, ¼ cup rosemary sprigs, 1 teaspoon frankincense tears (if available), an assortment of colorful yellow and orange dried flowers, and about 1 teaspoon of a fixative such as orrisroot. Mix well.

Decorate the surface of the potpourri with small pomanders made from 2 or 3 lemons or hardy trifoliate oranges (inedible) studded with cloves. Score the rind lightly with a knife and then roll fruit in a half-and-half mixture of powdered orrisroot (to hold scent) and powdered ginger. Wipe off excess and insert cloves.

For apple-evergreen potpourri, score the outside of an apple and roll in a half-and-half mixture of orrisroot and cinnamon/allspice. Dust

Above: Orrisroot, far right, is used to hold the scent of dried flowers and herbs. To freshen last year's potpourri, add a few drops of a fragrant oil, such as rose or cinnamon, to a small portion of orrisroot and crush it in a mortar. Sprinkle this scented powder on a

Left: Set a scented, stylish scene with a potpourri-filled velvet party purse. Dried garden flowers will be a welcome reminder of spring when winter winds blow.

clean and stud with cloves. Add ½ cup apple peels rolled in the same mixture. Add cinnamon sticks brushed with cinnamon oil, ¼ cup dried hibiscus blossoms (if available, to add color and a fruity note), ½ cup fresh cinnamon-basil sprigs for additional fragrance (if available), and staghorn sumac berries for color.

For rose petal potpourri, start with a purchased floral potpourri and then decorate the surface of the potpourri with dried rosebuds and an assortment of other dried flowers such as globe amaranth, cockscomb, lamb's ears, silver king artemisia, and rose geranium leaves.

Left: Soak a crocheted doily in diluted white glue or liquid laundry starch. Shape doily around a glass to make a textured container.

Drying Hint

A microwave oven will dry herbs and flowers quickly. Place petals and leaves in a microwave-safe container and cover with silica gel. Put a small cup of water in the oven with the container. Microwave at LOW 1 to 4 minutes, checking each minute to see if dry. Dried materials will be fragile, but smooth.

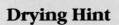

Above: Christmas hankies from the 1940s and 1950s can be found at antique shops and yard sales. They make sweet sachets when filled with a homemade potpourri.

less-than-fresh batch of blossoms to wake them up.
Make a fresh batch of potpourri by following the recipes on these pages. Or let your flower garden inspire you. Clockwise from left: rose petal potpourri, apple-evergreen potpourri, and citrus-evergreen potpourri.

A Country Christmas Pantry

THE PERFECT GIFT: CHOCOLATE

♥

BAKE A BATCH OF
CITRUS TREATS

♥

SHARE THE SWEETNESS

♥

O CHRISTMAS CHEESE!

♥

HOMESPUN DESSERTS

♥

IDEAS: EASYGOING
ENTERTAINING

The Perfect Gift: Chocolate

A gift of mouth-watering chocolate comes to mind for many occasions, especially romantic ones, such as Valentine's Day, a birthday, or an anniversary. Now you can roll all of these holidays into one sweet event. Use these luscious chocolate gift ideas to create a very special Christmas.

Outa-This-World Hot Fudge Sauce

½ cup whipping cream
¼ cup butter or margarine
½ cup firmly packed brown sugar
⅓ cup sugar
⅛ teaspoon salt
½ cup cocoa
1 tablespoon brandy (optional)
1 teaspoon vanilla extract
Ice cream

Combine first 2 ingredients in a small saucepan; cook over medium heat until butter melts. Bring to a boil; stir in sugars and salt. Cook over medium heat, stirring constantly, until sugar dissolves. Remove from heat; stir in cocoa with a wire whisk until blended. Stir in brandy, if desired, and vanilla.

Serve immediately over ice cream, or cool to room temperature; cover tightly and refrigerate. Yield: 1¼ cups.

Note: Present this gift with ice-cream scoop and instructions for heating sauce.

Directions for heating: 1) Microwave fudge sauce in a small glass bowl at HIGH for 1½ minutes, stirring every 30 seconds. 2) Or, place sauce in a small saucepan, and cook over low heat, stirring frequently. 3) Or, place sauce in top of a double boiler; bring water to a boil. Reduce heat, simmering until thoroughly heated.

Praline Truffles

10 ounces bittersweet chocolate, cut into ¼″ pieces
½ cup whipping cream
2 tablespoons powdered sugar
2 egg yolks
1½ tablespoons praline liqueur
Finely crushed chocolate wafer cookies, finely chopped hazelnuts, or cocoa

---

Holiday Gift-Wrap Suggestions

A little time is all it takes to create these easy-to-finish wraps for fabulous food gifts. Small wooden bandboxes embellished by your favorite painting technique make pretty, yet practical, containers. Or, cover the top of a gift box with a scrap of lace for an elegant touch. By wrapping the bottom and the top separately, the box can be used again and again long after the sweet treats are gone.

Design your own gift wrap with the help of a color copy machine. (Call your local print shop to find such a copier.) Simply photocopy a design onto white paper (reduce or enlarge the pattern as desired) to create wrapping paper for a small gift box. You can achieve a dramatic two-color effect by pairing colored paper stock with your red or green printed design.

Jar toppers can be created in the same way. After copying, center the jar lid over the design and lightly trace around the lid. With the design centered, cut a circle twice the diameter of the lid.

To make sharp pleats for a very neat fit, score the outer edges of the jar topper up to the traced circle in a spoke-like fashion with scissors. Place the jar topper on the lid, fold pleats, and tie with yarn or ribbon.

Place chocolate pieces in top of a double boiler; bring water to a boil. Reduce heat to low; cook until chocolate melts.

Add whipping cream and sugar to chocolate; cook over low heat, stirring constantly, until chocolate mixture is thoroughly heated and smooth. Remove from heat and cool 5 minutes.

Add egg yolks, one at a time, beating well with a wire whisk after each addition. Stir in praline liqueur.

Pour chocolate mixture into a medium bowl; cover and chill at least 1 hour.

Shape chocolate mixture into 1″ balls. Roll

Above: A homemade gift of chocolate will light up a certain someone's eyes, especially when it is presented in a carefully selected gift wrap. Try the elegance of a few unshelled pecans painted with gold ink to adorn a bottle of Chocolate Liqueur. Or create a personalized jar topper for the Cinnamon-Almond Mocha Mix—a simple, sure sign of affection. In the foreground, from left, are Praline Truffles and Outa-This-World Hot Fudge Sauce.

truffles in your choice of cookie crumbs, hazelnuts, or cocoa. Cover and chill until firm. Store in refrigerator up to 1 week or freeze up to 2 months. Yield: about 5 dozen.

Chocolate Liqueur

1½ cups sugar
¾ cup water
3 cups vodka
¼ cup plus 1 tablespoon cocoa
1 (6") vanilla bean, split lengthwise

Combine sugar and water in a medium saucepan. Bring to a boil over medium heat, stirring occasionally, until sugar dissolves. Remove from heat; let cool completely. Add vodka and cocoa to sugar mixture; stir with a wire whisk until well blended. Pour mixture into a glass jar and add vanilla bean. Cover tightly, and store in a cool, dark place for 14 days, shaking thoroughly each day. Remove and discard vanilla bean.

Place a coffee filter in a large metal strainer; strain vodka mixture into a sterilized glass jar. (Straining process will take at least 8 hours.) Cover tightly and let stand in a cool, dark place for at least 30 days. Yield: about 1 quart.

Choclava

1 (16-ounce) package frozen commercial
   phyllo pastry, thawed
1 cup butter or margarine, melted
1½ cups finely chopped pecans or walnuts
¾ cup semisweet chocolate mini-morsels
2 tablespoons sugar
½ teaspoon ground cinnamon
Syrup (recipe follows)
¼ cup semisweet chocolate mini-morsels,
   melted

Cut phyllo sheets to fit a 15" x 10" x 1" jelly-roll pan. Butter pan. Layer 4 phyllo sheets in pan, brushing each sheet with melted butter. Cover. Set aside. Keep remaining phyllo covered.

Combine pecans and next 3 ingredients in a small bowl, stirring well. Sprinkle ½ cup pecan mixture over phyllo in pan. Top pecan mixture with 4 sheets of phyllo, brushing each sheet with butter. Repeat procedure with remaining pecan mixture, phyllo, and butter, ending with buttered phyllo. Score top layer of pastry into about 72 diamond shapes, cutting to, but not through, fourth sheet of phyllo. (See Diagram.) Bake at 350° for 35 minutes. Cut all the way through diamond shapes. Drizzle warm syrup over pastries. Cool on wire rack. Transfer to serving platter. Pipe melted chocolate over pastries in desired design, using metal tip No. 3. Yield: about 6 dozen.

Syrup:

¾ cup honey
¼ cup plus 2 tablespoons sugar
¼ cup plus 2 tablespoons water
1 tablespoon freshly squeezed lemon juice
1 (3½") stick cinnamon
½ teaspoon whole cloves
1 teaspoon vanilla extract

Combine first 6 ingredients in a medium saucepan. Bring to a boil; reduce heat and simmer 8 minutes. Remove from heat; remove and discard spices. Stir in vanilla. Yield: 1⅓ cups.

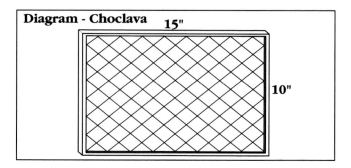

Cinnamon-Almond Mocha Mix

1 (6-ounce) jar powdered nondairy coffee
   creamer
1 cup plus 2 tablespoons sifted powdered
   sugar
½ cup instant coffee granules
½ cup cocoa
2 teaspoons ground cinnamon
1 teaspoon almond extract
⅛ teaspoon salt

Combine all ingredients, stirring until well blended. Store at room temperature in an airtight container. To serve, spoon 2 to 3 tablespoons mocha mix into a mug; fill with boiling water. Stir well. Yield: about 3½ cups.

Opposite: Sweeten the holidays with, clockwise from top left, Choclava, Peanutty Chocolate Apples, Double-Boost Brownies, Choclava, and Coconut Gems.

84

Time and experience have conclusively proved that chocolate, when carefully prepared, is a wholesome form of food. It is very suitable for persons faced with great mental exertion, preachers, lawyers, and above all travelers.

—Jean-Anthelme Brillat-Savarin
from *The Physiology of Taste,* 1825

Festive Glittery Garland

Make yards and yards of glittery garland (shown on pages 80 and 81) from a single roll of colored foil paper. Check with your nearest candy-making supply shop to find foil paper.

To make a garland with accordion pleats, fanfold a long 1"-wide strip of foil. Tape ends of additional strips together to make the garland longer. (Handle carefully. This thin foil tears easily.)

To make the diamond garland, fold a long 1½"-wide strip of foil in half to measure ¾" wide. With scissors, make evenly spaced cuts along the length. (See Diagram 1.) Unfold foil and then *gently* pull strip to open garland. (See Diagram 2.)

Our gilded nuts on pages 80 and 81 are made by covering unshelled walnuts and pecans with gold foil wrappers that were saved from small candies. Sprinkle a handful of these wherever you need some holiday sparkle.

Diamond Garland

Fold

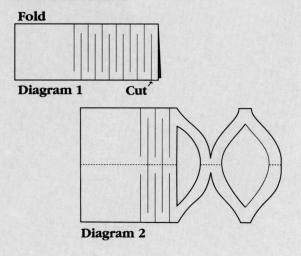

Diagram 1   **Cut**

Diagram 2

Double-Boost Brownies

1 cup sugar
½ cup butter or margarine
¼ cup water
¼ cup light corn syrup
1 (12-ounce) package semisweet chocolate morsels
1 teaspoon vanilla extract
3 eggs
6 ounces bittersweet chocolate, cut into ¼" pieces
1¼ cups all-purpose flour
¼ teaspoon baking powder
¼ teaspoon baking soda
⅛ teaspoon salt
1 cup coarsely chopped walnuts
3 ounces white chocolate, cut into ¼" pieces

Cut a piece of 12"-wide aluminum foil 21" long; fold lengthwise into thirds. Butter one side of foil; place lengthwise, greased side up, in a buttered 13" x 9" x 2" baking pan, allowing foil to extend 2" beyond ends of pan. Fold overhanging foil down over ends of pan.

Combine sugar, butter, water, and corn syrup in a large saucepan; bring to a boil over medium heat, stirring frequently, until sugar dissolves. Remove from heat; add chocolate morsels and vanilla. Let stand 1 to 2 minutes. Stir with a wire whisk until smooth. Add eggs, one at a time, beating well after each addition. Stir in bittersweet chocolate pieces. Combine flour and next 3 ingredients; add dry ingredients, walnuts, and white chocolate pieces to chocolate mixture, stirring well.

Pour batter into prepared pan. Bake at 325° for 45 to 50 minutes. Cool completely on a wire rack; then cut into squares.

Using extended pieces of foil as handles, lift brownies from pan. Remove and discard foil. Store brownies at room temperature in an airtight container. Yield: 2 dozen.

Peanutty Chocolate Apples

12 to 14 medium apples
Wooden skewers
1 (12-ounce) package peanut butter morsels
⅔ cup sifted powdered sugar
⅔ cup cocoa
½ cup vegetable oil
1½ cups chopped unsalted peanuts, toasted

Wash and dry apples; remove stems. Insert a wooden skewer into stem end of each apple. Set aside.

Combine peanut butter morsels and next 3 ingredients in top of a double boiler; bring water to a boil. Reduce heat to low. Stir gently until morsels melt and mixture is smooth. Remove from heat and cool slightly.

Place chopped peanuts in a small bowl. Quickly dip apples in chocolate mixture; allow excess mixture to drip back into pan. Dip chocolate-covered apples in nuts, coating bottom third of apple. Place on lightly buttered baking sheets to cool. Yield: 12 to 14 servings.

Coconut Gems

½ cup butter or margarine, softened
1½ cups sifted powdered sugar
1 egg
1 teaspoon vanilla extract
1¼ cups all-purpose flour
⅓ cup cocoa
½ teaspoon baking soda
½ teaspoon salt
Coconut Filling (recipe follows)

Cream butter; gradually add sugar, beating at medium speed of an electric mixer. Add egg and vanilla; beat well. Combine flour, cocoa, soda, and salt; add to creamed mixture, beating just until blended. Cover and chill 2 hours. Divide dough in half. Place each portion of dough between 2 sheets of plastic wrap. Roll each portion of dough out to a 9½" x 6" rectangle. (Dough will be soft.) Remove plastic wrap.

Divide coconut filling in half. Shape each portion into a 9½" log. Place long edge of 1 coconut roll about ½" from long edge of 1 chocolate rectangle, and roll up jellyroll fashion. Repeat for remaining roll. Wrap rolls in wax paper and chill 8 hours.

Cut each roll into ¼" slices. Place slices on lightly greased cookie sheets and bake at 350° for 6 to 8 minutes. Cool slightly on cookie sheets. Remove to wire racks and cool completely. Yield: 4 dozen.

Coconut Filling:

1 (3-ounce) package cream cheese, softened
½ cup sifted powdered sugar
2 tablespoons all-purpose flour
1 teaspoon vanilla extract
1 cup shredded coconut
½ cup finely chopped pecans

Beat cream cheese at medium speed of an electric mixer; gradually add sugar, beating until light and fluffy. Add flour and vanilla; beat well. Stir in coconut and pecans. Cover and chill thoroughly. Yield: about 1½ cups.

Toffee Trail Mix

10 cups popped corn
1 cup dry-roasted salted peanuts
1 cup candy-coated chocolate pieces
1 cup raisins
2⅔ cups sugar
1½ cups butter
⅔ cup firmly packed brown sugar
½ cup water
½ teaspoon salt
1 tablespoon vanilla extract

Combine popped corn, peanuts, chocolate pieces, and raisins in a large bowl; toss well to combine.

Combine sugar and next 4 ingredients in a large saucepan; cook over low heat, stirring gently, until butter melts. Cook over medium heat, without stirring, to hard crack stage (300°). Remove from heat; stir in vanilla.

Carefully pour hot toffee mixture over popcorn mixture, stirring well with a wooden spoon. Spoon coated popcorn onto baking sheets. Flatten mixture to ¾" thickness. Cool 15 minutes or until firm.

Break the popcorn mixture into bite-size pieces. Store in an airtight container up to 2 weeks. Yield: 16 cups.

Bake a Batch of Citrus Treats

Bring the tangy taste of oranges, lemons, and limes to your table this holiday season. These refreshing recipes will contrast nicely with the sweeter, richer foods of the season.

Lemony Almond Cake

1 cup butter or margarine, softened
1 cup sugar
4 eggs
½ teaspoon grated lemon rind
¼ cup plus 1 tablespoon freshly squeezed
  lemon juice, divided
2¼ cups sifted cake flour
½ teaspoon cream of tartar
½ teaspoon salt
1 cup blanched slivered almonds, toasted
  and divided
1 teaspoon vanilla extract
½ cup sifted powdered sugar

Cream butter; gradually add sugar, beating well at medium speed of an electric mixer. Add eggs, one at a time, beating after each addition. Add lemon rind and 2 tablespoons lemon juice, beating well.

Combine flour, cream of tartar, and salt; gradually add to creamed mixture, 1 cup at a time, beating at low speed just until blended. Stir in ¾ cup almonds and vanilla.

Pour batter into a greased and floured 9″ x 5″ x 3″ loafpan. Sprinkle with remaining ¼ cup almonds. Bake at 325° for 1 hour or until a wooden pick inserted in center comes out clean.

Combine sifted powdered sugar and remaining 3 tablespoons juice in a small saucepan; cook over medium heat until sugar dissolves, stirring frequently. Pour glaze over hot cake slowly,

Opposite: From dinner rolls to dessert, lemons and oranges add tangy refreshment to the menu. Clockwise from top: Orange Rum Rolls in the Grapevine Heart Basket, Lemony Almond Cake, and Orange Florentines. Instructions for the basket are on page 90.

allowing glaze to soak into cake. Cool in pan 10 to 15 minutes; remove from pan and let cool completely on a wire rack. Yield: 1 loaf.

Orange Florentines

⅔ cup sugar
½ cup butter
2 tablespoons milk
2 tablespoons light corn syrup
⅓ cup all-purpose flour
¼ cup Candied Orange Rind (recipe follows)
¾ cup sliced blanched almonds
1 teaspoon vanilla extract
⅔ cup semisweet chocolate morsels, melted

Line baking sheets with aluminum foil, keeping foil smooth.

Combine first 4 ingredients in a heavy saucepan. Cook over low heat, stirring gently, until sugar dissolves. Cook over medium heat, without stirring, until mixture reaches thread stage (232°). Remove from heat and stir in flour and next 3 ingredients.

Drop dough by teaspoonfuls, 4″ apart, onto prepared baking sheets. Bake at 350° for 6 to 8 minutes or until light caramel color. Cool completely on baking sheets on a wire rack. Carefully remove cookies from aluminum foil.

Spread a thin layer of melted chocolate on flat side of 1 cookie, leaving a ¼″ margin around edges. Gently press on another cookie, flat side toward chocolate, forming a sandwich. Chill cookies 20 to 30 minutes. Yield: 1½ dozen.

Candied Orange Rind:

½ cup (⅛″-wide) strips orange rind (1 large
  orange)
½ cup water
¼ cup sugar

Cut orange rind strips into ½″ pieces. Combine water and sugar in a small nonaluminum saucepan; bring to a boil over medium heat, stirring constantly, until sugar dissolves. Add orange rind pieces. Cook over low heat until all liquid has been absorbed. Transfer orange rind to wax paper with a fork; separate into individual pieces. Cool completely. Store in an airtight container for 1 to 2 months. Yield: ⅓ cup.

Orange Rum Rolls

⅔ cup butter or margarine
½ cup sugar
1 teaspoon grated orange rind
¼ cup freshly squeezed orange juice
1½ teaspoons salt
½ teaspoon orange extract
2 packages dry yeast
¾ cup warm water (105° to 115°)
8 to 8½ cups all-purpose flour, divided
5 eggs, slightly beaten
2 tablespoons butter or margarine, melted
Orange Rum Glaze (recipe follows)

Combine butter, sugar, orange rind, orange juice, salt, and orange extract in a saucepan; heat until butter melts, stirring occasionally. Cool to 105° to 115°.

Dissolve yeast in warm water in a large bowl; let stand 5 minutes. Stir in orange mixture, 3 cups flour, and eggs; beat at medium speed of an electric mixer until well blended. Gradually stir in enough flour to make a soft dough.

Turn dough out onto a generously floured surface and knead until smooth and elastic (about 5 minutes). Place in a well-greased bowl, turning to grease top. Cover and let rise in a warm place (85°), free from drafts, 1 hour or until doubled in bulk.

Punch dough down; cover and let rise for 30 more minutes or until doubled in bulk.

Punch dough down; turn out onto a generously floured surface. Divide dough in half. Roll 1 portion of dough into a 14″ x 12″ rectangle. Brush with melted butter.

Fold rectangle into thirds to resemble a folded letter. Cut crosswise into 1″ strips. Twist ends of each strip in opposite directions. Stretch twisted strip slightly, and tie in a loose knot; tuck ends under.

Repeat procedure with remaining half of dough. Place on greased baking sheets.

Let rise in a warm place (85°), uncovered and free from drafts, 30 minutes or until doubled in bulk. Bake at 375° for 20 minutes or until golden brown. Cool slightly and brush with Orange Rum Glaze. Yield: 2 dozen.

Grapevine Heart Basket

A ruffled basket filled with Orange Rum Rolls adds a country touch to any table setting.

Materials:
pattern on page 147
⅓ yard (45″-wide) red-and-white
    miniplaid
matching thread
1 (11″-diameter) grapevine heart basket
    with 5″ depth
hot-glue gun and glue sticks
scrap of brown felt
matching thread
polyester stuffing
1 (¼″) red heart button
½ yard (1/16″-wide) green satin ribbon
½ yard (1½″-wide) red-and-green striped
    grosgrain ribbon
2 (½″) brass bells

Note: All seam allowances are ¼″.
Cut 2 (5″ x 40″) strips from miniplaid.

With right sides facing, stitch 5″ ends of strips together to make a circle. To hem, fold under ¼″ twice all around 1 long edge and stitch. Fold under 1¼″ all around other edge and press. Run a gathering stitch ¾″ from this folded edge.

With wrong side of fabric against outside of basket, match 1 seam to top center of heart and 1 seam to point of heart, adjusting gathers to fit. With top edges even, glue fabric to basket along gathering stitch.

Using pattern, cut 2 gingerbread men from felt. Place pieces together and whipstitch edges, leaving small opening in head. Stuff firmly. Whipstitch opening closed. Glue on heart button. (See photograph on page 88.) Using 5″ of satin ribbon, tie small bow and glue to center of gingerbread man's neck. Trim ends of ribbon.

Tie grosgrain ribbon into a bow; notch ends. Tie 1 bell to each end of remaining satin ribbon. Tie ribbon around center of bow, allowing bells to hang loosely. Glue bow to fabric at top center of basket. Glue gingerbread man to center of bow.

Orange Rum Glaze:

¾ cup sifted powdered sugar
3 tablespoons orange marmalade
1 to 2 teaspoons dark rum

Combine powdered sugar, orange marmalade, and dark rum in a small bowl; stir until smooth. Yield: ⅓ cup.

Angel Lime Torte

2 egg whites
½ teaspoon cream of tartar
¼ teaspoon salt
1 cup sugar, divided
4 egg yolks
1 tablespoon grated lime rind
¼ cup freshly squeezed lime juice
⅛ teaspoon salt
1 cup whipping cream, whipped
Sweetened whipped cream
Fresh lime slices

Beat egg whites (at room temperature), cream of tartar, and salt at high speed of an electric mixer just until foamy. Gradually add ½ cup sugar, 1 tablespoon at a time, beating until stiff peaks form and sugar dissolves (2 to 4 minutes).

Pipe or spread meringue onto a baking sheet lined with parchment paper. Using the back of a spoon, shape meringue into an 8″ circle; shape the circle into a shell to hold lime mixture. (Sides should be about 1¾″ high.) Bake at 275° for 1 hour. Turn oven off, and cool shell in oven 2 hours. Carefully peel paper from shell and cool completely on a wire rack. Set aside.

Beat egg yolks in top of a double boiler until thick and lemon colored; gradually add remaining ½ cup sugar, beating well. Stir in lime rind, lime juice, and salt. Place over simmering water and cook 8 to 10 minutes or until lime mixture is thick. Transfer lime mixture to a large bowl and cool completely.

Gently fold whipped cream into lime mixture; spoon into prepared meringue shell. Cover and chill at least 8 hours. Garnish with sweetened whipped cream and fresh lime slices. Yield: 8 servings.

Country Orange Chess Pie

4 eggs, slightly beaten
1½ cups sugar
¼ cup half-and-half
¼ cup butter or margarine, melted
2 teaspoons grated orange rind
¼ cup freshly squeezed orange juice
2 tablespoons cornmeal
1 tablespoon all-purpose flour
1 unbaked 9″ pastry shell
Orange wedges (optional)

Combine eggs, sugar, half-and-half, butter, orange rind, orange juice, cornmeal, and flour in a large mixing bowl, stirring well to combine. Pour mixture into unbaked pastry shell. Bake at 350° for 45 to 50 minutes or until set. Cool completely on a wire rack. Garnish with orange wedges, if desired. Yield: one 9″ pie.

Lemon Bars

3 cups all-purpose flour, divided
⅔ cup sifted powdered sugar
1 cup butter or margarine
¾ teaspoon baking soda
2 cups sugar
5 eggs, slightly beaten
½ teaspoon grated lemon rind
¼ cup plus 2 tablespoons freshly squeezed
  lemon juice
Additional powdered sugar

Combine 2½ cups flour and ⅔ cup powdered sugar; cut in butter with pastry blender until mixture resembles coarse meal.

Spoon flour mixture into a lightly greased 15″ x 10″ x 1″ jellyroll pan; press firmly and evenly into pan, using fingertips. Bake at 350° for 20 to 25 minutes or until lightly browned.

Combine remaining ½ cup flour and soda; set aside. Combine sugar and next 3 ingredients; stir well. Stir dry ingredients into egg mixture. Spoon into baked crust.

Bake at 350° for 30 minutes or until lightly browned and set. Cool completely on a wire rack. Remove from pan. Dust lightly with additional powdered sugar and cut into bars. Yield: 6 dozen.

Before the days of commercial shipping, oranges, lemons, and limes didn't grace fruit baskets year-round as they do now. Some people tasted citrus only once a year—Christmastime. The Tiny Citrus Tarts and Angel Lime Torte, above, will give a rare, fresh finale to any meal.

Tiny Citrus Tarts

½ cup butter
3 ounces lemon- or orange-flavored
   Neufchâtel, softened
1 cup all-purpose flour
Fresh Lemon Curd (recipe follows)
Fresh Orange Cream (recipe follows)
Sweetened whipped cream and fresh fruit
   (optional)

Cream butter; add Neufchâtel, beating well at medium speed of an electric mixer. Add all-purpose flour, beating well. Shape dough into a ball. Chill 1 hour.

Divide dough evenly into 24 balls. Roll each ball into a 4" circle between 2 sheets of heavy-duty plastic wrap. Remove plastic wrap and fit circles into 3" tart pans; trim edges as needed.

Prick bottom and sides of pastries with a fork. Bake at 375° for 8 to 10 minutes or until lightly browned. Remove from pans; let cool completely on wire racks.

Spoon Fresh Lemon Curd into half of pastries; spoon Fresh Orange Cream into remaining half of pastries. Garnish with whipped cream and fruit, if desired. Yield: 24 servings.

Fresh Lemon Curd:

½ cup sugar
1 teaspoon cornstarch
3 egg yolks
2 eggs
1 teaspoon grated lemon rind
½ cup freshly squeezed lemon juice
¼ cup plus 2 tablespoons butter or
   margarine, cut into small pieces

Combine sugar and cornstarch in top of a nonaluminum double boiler; stir well. Add egg yolks, eggs, grated lemon rind, and lemon juice; beat well with a wire whisk. Cook over simmering water, stirring constantly, until smooth and thick. Remove from heat; add butter, stirring until butter melts.

Place plastic wrap directly on top of lemon curd; chill thoroughly. Yield: 1⅓ cups.

Note: Fresh Lemon Curd may also be served with English Tea Scones shown on page 115.

Fresh Orange Cream:

3 tablespoons sugar
2½ teaspoons cornstarch
Pinch of salt
¾ cup whipping cream
½ teaspoon grated orange rind
¼ cup freshly squeezed orange juice
3 egg yolks
2 tablespoons butter or margarine
½ teaspoon vanilla extract

Combine sugar, cornstarch, and salt in a medium nonaluminum saucepan; stir well. Add whipping cream, grated orange rind, orange juice, and egg yolks; beat well with a wire whisk. Cook, stirring constantly, over medium-low heat until smooth and thick. Remove from heat; add butter and vanilla, stirring until butter melts.

Place plastic wrap directly on top of orange cream; chill thoroughly. Yield: 1¼ cups.

Note: Fresh Orange Cream may also be served with English Tea Scones shown on page 115.

Lemon Puffed Pancake

½ cup all-purpose flour
½ cup milk
2 eggs, beaten
1 teaspoon grated lemon rind
1 teaspoon freshly squeezed lemon juice
½ teaspoon vanilla extract
¼ teaspoon salt
Pinch of nutmeg
2 tablespoons butter or margarine
1 tablespoon powdered sugar
Orange marmalade

Combine all-purpose flour, milk, eggs, grated lemon rind, lemon juice, vanilla, salt, and nutmeg in a medium mixing bowl; beat at medium speed of an electric mixer just until blended. Batter will be lumpy. Chill at least 1 hour.

Melt butter in a 9" round cakepan. Pour chilled batter into cakepan. Bake at 450° for 10 minutes. Reduce heat to 350° and bake an additional 10 minutes. Remove from pan. Sprinkle with powdered sugar and serve immediately with orange marmalade. Yield: 4 servings.

Share the Sweetness

The trace of an herb or blossom scent can add a sweet mystery to even a basic recipe. When used in baking, these flavored sugars and syrups will make the scents and tastes of rose geranium, mint, rose petals, and lemon verbena your personal secret ingredient.

For information about ordering herb plants and fresh cut herbs, see the source listing on page 154.

Rose Geranium Sugar

2 cups sugar
4 (2") rose geranium leaves (void of commercial insecticides)
2 to 4 drops red food coloring

Position knife blade in food processor bowl; add sugar and rose geranium leaves. Process 15 to 20 seconds or until leaves are minced. Slowly add food coloring through food chute with processor running; process just until well blended.

Spread sugar in a thin layer on a baking sheet; let stand at room temperature at least 8 hours or until dry. Before baking, top sugar cookies with Rose Geranium Sugar. Yield: 2 cups.

Maple Syrup Candies

1½ cups sugar
¼ cup maple syrup

Combine ingredients in a small bowl; stir until sugar is moistened. Press mixture firmly into 1" rubber candy molds; let stand at room temperature at least 8 hours or until dry. Remove from molds. Serve in hot tea. Yield: 2½ dozen.

Mint-Flavored Sugar Cubes

1 (16-ounce) package sugar cubes, divided
4 cups loosely packed mint sprigs, divided

Place a third of sugar cubes in a single layer in shallow container; top with half of mint. Repeat procedure with another third of sugar cubes and other half of mint.

Top with the remaining third of sugar cubes. Cover tightly and let stand at room temperature 4 to 5 days. Remove and discard mint. (Bottom sugar cubes will be very soft.) Place sugar cubes on a paper towel; let stand at room temperature at least 4 hours to dry. Store in an airtight container. Serve in hot tea. Yield: about 16 dozen.

Crystallized Pansies

1 egg white
1 dozen pansies (void of commercial insecticides)
½ cup superfine sugar

Beat egg white (at room temperature) until foamy. Brush each pansy petal with egg white. Sprinkle sugar over petal. Separate petals. Place on a wire rack and let stand at room temperature at least 8 hours or until dry. Garnish holiday desserts with Crystallized Pansies. Yield: 1 dozen.

Layered Lemon Verbena Sugar

3 cups sugar, divided
1 cup loosely packed lemon verbena leaves, divided (void of commercial insecticides)

Pour 1 cup sugar into a 1-quart glass jar. Add ½ cup lemon verbena. Repeat procedure with another cup sugar and ½ cup lemon verbena. Top with remaining cup of sugar. Cover tightly; let stand at room temperature at least 48 hours. Remove and discard lemon verbena. Yield: 3 cups.
Note: Layered Lemon Verbena Sugar can be substituted for plain sugar in sauces or desserts.

Rose Petal Syrup

1 dozen fresh red roses (void of commercial insecticides)
2 cups sugar, divided
½ cup water
1 tablespoon lemon juice
1 drop red food coloring (optional)

Separate roses into petals; wash petals and pat dry with paper towels. Carefully remove and discard white portion at base of each petal. (The white portion will cause the syrup to be bitter.)

Divide sugar in thirds, and sprinkle a third in bottom of an airtight container; cover with a thin layer of petals. Repeat procedure with another third of sugar and remaining petals. Top with remaining sugar. Cover and let stand at room temperature 48 hours or until sugar partially dissolves.

Remove and discard all petals. Transfer sugar to small saucepan; add water and cook over

Above: These aromatic confections will impart the flavors of herbs and flowers to cookies, cakes, biscuits, and even a soothing hot cup of tea. Clockwise from top left: Maple Syrup Candies, Rose Petal Syrup, Crystallized Pansies, and Rose Geranium Sugar.

medium heat, stirring constantly, until sugar dissolves. Remove from heat; cool completely and add lemon juice. Add food coloring, if desired. Store in an airtight container. Serve warm over pancakes or waffles. Yield: 2½ to 3 cups.

95

Canning Jar Recipe Holder

From its strawberry-studded lid to its handy front pocket, this recipe holder is as useful as it is pleasing. Tack it up on your pantry door for a decorative touch. It's a handy way to keep holiday recipes together.

With the addition of a few favorite preserve or jelly recipes, the soft, lace-trimmed canning jar becomes a gift with lasting benefits. To make this gift extra-special, add a pinch of potpourri or cinnamon chips when stuffing the jar lid.

Materials:
pattern on page 152
2 (7″ x 10″) pieces of posterboard
2 (7″ x 10″) pieces of craft fleece
craft glue or hot-glue gun with glue sticks
⅓ yard (45″-wide) red pindot
5″ x 8″ piece of red-and-green print
  (for jar lid)
7″ (½″-wide) pregathered eyelet trim
small amount of stuffing (for jar lid)
22″ (³⁄₁₆″-wide) green satin picot ribbon

Transfer jar pattern to 1 piece of posterboard and to fleece. Cut 1 from posterboard and 2 from fleece. Glue 2 fleece pieces to 1 side of the posterboard piece. Transfer placement line for jar front fabric to top piece of fleece.

For jar back, trace jar pattern on red pindot and cut out, adding ½″ seam allowance all around. Set aside. From pindot, cut 1 (7¼″) square for jar front and 1 (7¼″ x 8½″) rectangle for pocket.

With wrong sides facing, fold pocket to measure 7¼″ x 4¼″. Press pocket. With raw edges aligned, place pocket on right side of jar front. (See photograph.) Baste raw edges of pocket to jar front.

Align and pin top raw edge of jar front square along jar front placement line on fleece jar. Clip curves. Fold edges of fabric to back of posterboard and glue in place.

Transfer pattern for jar lid to red-and-green print and cut out. Turn straight edge of fabric under ¼″, and glue eyelet trim to this turned-under edge. (See photograph.)

Glue a small amount of stuffing on top of fleece at jar lid for extra padding.

Place the jar lid fabric right side up on top of the jar. Clip curves, fold the edges of the fabric to the back of the posterboard, and glue in place. Glue the straight edge of the eyelet-trimmed jar lid fabric to the pindot jar front. (See photograph.)

Transfer jar pattern to remaining posterboard and cut out ⅛″ inside pattern lines.

Center jar back right side up on posterboard shape. Clip curves, fold fabric edges to back, and glue in place.

With wrong sides facing, glue jar back to front.

Tie the ribbon in a bow around the neck of the jar.

O Christmas Cheese!

A variety of delicious cheeses enhances any party appetizer tray. The recipes here boast a dozen different cheese choices, from familiar Cheddar to pungent Asiago. Try the Appetizer Cheddar Cheesecake for a rich, garlic surprise. Or serve Rolled Chili Rellenos for an even spicier beginning. Whichever you choose, these cheese dishes are sure to please.

Savory Zucchini with Asiago and Cheddar

3 medium zucchini
¼ cup chopped onion
1 clove garlic, minced
2 teaspoons vegetable oil
⅔ cup commercial cornbread stuffing mix
½ cup (2 ounces) finely shredded Cheddar cheese
1 teaspoon chopped fresh parsley
¾ teaspoon minced fresh thyme
¼ teaspoon salt
¼ teaspoon pepper
¼ cup grated Asiago cheese
Fresh thyme sprigs

Cut zucchini crosswise into 1″ slices. Scoop out center of slices, leaving a ¼″ shell. Set zucchini shells aside.

Chop ¼ cup zucchini pulp. Discard remaining pulp. Sauté onion, garlic, and reserved pulp in oil in a small skillet until vegetables are tender and all liquid has been absorbed. Remove from heat and cool 5 minutes.

Combine onion mixture, stuffing mix, Cheddar cheese, parsley, thyme, salt, and pepper in a medium bowl; stir well.

Fill reserved zucchini shells with cheese mixture. Arrange on an ungreased baking sheet. Bake at 350° for 15 minutes. Remove from oven and sprinkle Asiago cheese evenly over filled zucchini shells. Bake an additional 3 minutes or until cheese melts. Transfer to a serving platter. Garnish with fresh thyme sprigs. Serve warm. Yield: about 1½ dozen appetizer servings.

Rolled Chili Rellenos

2 cups (8 ounces) shredded Monterey Jack cheese
3 (4-ounce) cans chopped green chilies, drained
2 eggs, slightly beaten
¼ teaspoon salt
¼ teaspoon ground cumin
⅛ teaspoon ground red pepper
1 (16-ounce) package frozen commercial phyllo pastry, thawed
¾ cup butter or margarine, melted

Combine first 6 ingredients in a medium bowl; stir well and set aside.

Cut phyllo lengthwise into 3 stacks of 4″-wide strips. Cover with a slightly damp towel. Discard remaining phyllo.

Layer 2 strips of phyllo, brushing each strip with melted butter. Place 1 tablespoon chili mixture at the bottom of pastry strip; fold bottom edge of phyllo over chili mixture. Fold sides over ½″. Roll up jellyroll fashion. Place roll, seam side down, on a lightly greased baking sheet. Repeat procedure with remaining phyllo, butter, and chili mixture. Bake at 375° for 30 minutes or until golden brown. Let cool for 15 minutes before serving. Yield: about 3 dozen appetizer servings.

Bubbling Bagel Bread

⅓ cup tomato paste
12 miniature bagels, cut in half
¾ cup (3 ounces) shredded mozzarella cheese
¼ cup plus 2 tablespoons mayonnaise
¼ teaspoon garlic powder
3 tablespoons freshly grated Parmesan cheese
⅓ cup sliced ripe olives (optional)

Spread tomato paste evenly on bagel halves; set aside. Combine mozzarella cheese, mayonnaise, and garlic powder in a small bowl; stir well. Spread cheese mixture over tomato paste. Sprinkle with Parmesan cheese. Top with olives, if desired. Place on an ungreased baking sheet; broil 4 inches from heat 3 to 5 minutes or until cheese melts. Yield: 24 appetizer servings.

Appetizer Cheddar Cheesecake

1 cup soft breadcrumbs, toasted
⅓ cup grated Parmesan cheese
¼ cup plus 1 tablespoon butter or
    margarine, melted
3 (8-ounce) packages cream cheese,
    softened
3 cups (12 ounces) shredded Cheddar
    cheese
1 cup small-curd cottage cheese
⅔ cup chopped green onions
3 tablespoons canned jalapeño pepper,
    seeded and chopped
2 tablespoons milk
1 clove garlic, minced
¾ teaspoon chili powder
4 eggs
Fresh jalapeño peppers and sweet red
    peppers, cut into holly leaf and berry
    shapes

Grease bottom and sides of a 9″ springform pan. Combine breadcrumbs, Parmesan cheese, and butter in a small bowl; stir well. Coat bottom and sides of greased pan with breadcrumb mixture. Bake at 350° for 8 to 10 minutes or until set; set aside.

Position knife blade in food processor bowl; add cream cheese. Process 1½ minutes or until smooth. Add Cheddar cheese and next 6 ingredients; process 2 minutes, scraping sides of processor bowl occasionally. Add eggs, one at a time, processing after each addition just until well blended. Pour cheese mixture into prepared pan. Bake at 325° for 1 hour and 15 minutes. Turn oven off, partially open oven door, and let cheesecake cool 1 hour. Transfer to a wire rack. Remove sides of springform pan. Garnish with jalapeño peppers and sweet red peppers. Cut cheesecake into thin wedges and serve with wheat crackers. Yield: one 9″ cheesecake.

Right: Whether you're throwing a party or just going to one, these cheesy appetizers will get things off to a great start. Counterclockwise from left: Rolled Chili Rellenos, Bubbling Bagel Bread, and Appetizer Cheddar Cheesecake.

Cheese in a Blanket

1 (17¼-ounce) package frozen commercial
   puff pastry, thawed
¼ cup plus 2 tablespoons coarse-grained
   mustard
1 small cooking apple, cored and thinly
   sliced
4 ounces prosciutto, cut into small pieces
1 (4″) wheel Brie cheese, cut into 18
   wedges
1 egg white, slightly beaten

Roll each pastry sheet to a 12″ square; cut
each 12″ square into 9 (4″) squares. Working
with 1 square at a time, spread 1 teaspoon mustard in center of pastry square. Top with a slice
of apple, a piece of prosciutto, and a wedge of
Brie; reserve remaining apple for other uses.
Brush edges of each pastry square with egg
white. Fold diagonally over prosciutto and
cheese, forming a triangle; press edges with a
fork dipped in flour. Place on ungreased baking
sheets. Bake at 425° for 20 minutes or until
golden brown. Transfer to a wire rack; cool to
room temperature. Yield: 18 appetizer servings.

Cheese Bites and Olives

12 ounces Muenster cheese, cut into ½″
   cubes
1 (8-ounce) jar Greek olives, drained
¼ cup plus 2 tablespoons tarragon
   vinegar
1 tablespoon Dijon mustard
3 cloves garlic, minced
½ teaspoon pepper
¼ teaspoon salt
1 cup olive oil
½ cup chopped fresh parsley

Arrange cheese and olives in a large shallow
dish; set aside. Combine vinegar and next 4 ingredients in a medium bowl; stir well. Gradually
add olive oil to vinegar mixture in a slow steady
stream, beating with a wire whisk. Stir in parsley. Pour mixture over cheese and olives; chill
at least 24 hours.
   Drain cheese and olives; transfer to a serving
platter and serve chilled. Yield: 24 appetizer
servings.

Brick and Blue Potatoes

24 (2¼ pounds) new potatoes
2 cups blue cheese, crumbled
½ cup sour cream
4 slices bacon, cooked and crumbled
⅛ teaspoon salt
⅛ teaspoon pepper
¼ cup (1 ounce) finely shredded brick or
   mozzarella cheese
Paprika

Wash potatoes; cook in boiling water to cover
15 to 20 minutes or until tender. Drain and
cool slightly. Cut potatoes in half. Scoop out
center of potatoes, leaving a ¼″ shell. Cut a thin
slice off bottom of each potato to level, if necessary. Set aside.
   Combine blue cheese and next 4 ingredients
in a medium bowl. Spoon cheese mixture evenly
into potato shells. Place filled potatoes on an ungreased baking sheet. Bake at 325° for 15 minutes. Remove from oven. Sprinkle brick or
mozzarella cheese evenly over filled potatoes.
Sprinkle with paprika; let stand at room temperature until cheese melts. Serve hot. Yield:
48 appetizer servings.

Pesto and Cheese Terrine

1 cup ricotta cheese
½ cup grated Parmesan cheese
½ cup chopped walnuts
1 teaspoon sugar
1 clove garlic, cut in half
14 ounces provolone cheese, cut into thin
   slices
1 (8-ounce) container commercial pesto
½ cup chopped sun-dried tomatoes packed
   in oil, drained
Fresh basil leaves and cherry tomatoes

Position knife blade in food processor bowl;
add first 5 ingredients. Process 2 minutes or
until well blended. Set aside.
   Lightly oil an 8½″ x 4½″ x 3″ loafpan. Cover
bottom and sides of loafpan with cheese slices,
allowing slices to overlap. Trim edges to fit pan.
Spread half of pesto over bottom layer of
cheese; sprinkle with a third of chopped tomato.
Cover with 1 layer of cheese slices, allowing

Pineapple-Cheese Welcome Spread

½ (8-ounce) package cream cheese, softened
2 tablespoons mayonnaise
2 (8-ounce) packages medium Cheddar cheese, shredded
¼ cup pineapple preserves
½ cup sliced almonds, toasted
1 (3-ounce) jar pimiento-stuffed olives, drained
1 small fresh pineapple frond

Position knife blade in food processor bowl; add cream cheese and mayonnaise. Process until mixture is smooth. Add Cheddar cheese in 2 to 3 batches, processing until smooth. Scrape sides of bowl with a spatula after processing each batch. Transfer mixture to a medium bowl and stir in preserves. Cover and refrigerate until thoroughly chilled.

Shape cheese mixture into an oval, molding to resemble a pineapple half; place on serving platter. Insert almonds into cheese in intersecting, diagonal 1″-wide rows to resemble the diamond-shaped cross-hatching on pineapples. (See photograph.) Cut olives crosswise into ⅛″-thick slices. Place olive slices on cheese between rows of almonds.

Cut a lengthwise slice off back of pineapple frond so that it will sit flat. Place frond, cut side down, on serving platter at top of cheese pineapple, pressing gently to attach. Trim excess leaves to achieve proper proportion, if necessary. Cover and store in refrigerator. Let stand at room temperature 10 minutes to soften before serving with assorted crackers. Yield: 6 cups.

edges to overlap. Trim edges to fit pan. Spread ricotta mixture over cheese slices; top with a third of chopped tomato. Cover with a single layer of cheese slices, allowing edges to overlap. Trim edges to fit pan. Spread remaining half of pesto over cheese slices and top with remaining third chopped tomato. Cover with a single layer of cheese, allowing edges to overlap. Trim edges to fit pan.

Cover tightly with plastic wrap, pressing firmly to compact loaf. Chill at least 8 hours.

Remove plastic wrap from loafpan and invert onto a serving platter. Garnish with basil leaves and cherry tomatoes. Cut into ½″ slices and serve with sliced and toasted Italian bread.
Yield: 16 appetizer servings.

Fruit Basket Ornaments

Turn an everyday basket into folk art stars. Use your imagination to combine and layer different shapes and colors and create a star-burst effect.

Materials for about 6 ornaments:
1 fruit basket
scissors or mat knife
watercolor paints: red, green
small watercolor brush
craft glue
2 yards (¹⁄₁₆″-wide) red or green satin ribbon

Remove wire handles from basket and discard. Cut top band from basket and discard. Unweave wooden slats and wet thoroughly. Using fingers, smooth and straighten slats. Allow to dry.

Using scissors, cut some slat strips into ¼″, ½″, and 1″ widths with lengths varying from 3″ to 5″. Apply red and green watercolor paints to some strips. Allow to dry. Cut some strips into desired accent shapes. (See photograph.)

Using as few as 4 or as many as 8 plain and painted strips, stack and glue strips into ornament shapes. Glue colored accent shapes on ornaments as desired. (See photograph.)

For hanger, knot ends of 1 (8″) length of ribbon and glue to back of 1 ornament. Or weave 1 (12″) length of ribbon over and under strips in 1 direction; reverse and weave back to starting point. Tie ribbon ends together at back of ornament and cut excess ribbon. Loop 1 (8″) length of matching ribbon under woven ribbon at back of ornament and knot ends together for hanger. Repeat to finish remaining ornaments.

Above: The Princess Fudge Fruitcake lets imaginative cooks create a favorite Christmas scene using the simplest of molds—cookie cutters. This winter forest is as simple—and delicious—as it looks.

Homespun Desserts

In the 15th century, Italy began importing a sweet sensation—sugar. Italian confectioners, who learned to spin this treat, were praised for the magnificent sculptures they made for the tables of the aristocracy.

Heads will spin when delicate spun sugar and caramelized sugar desserts come out of your kitchen this Christmas. These recipes range from rudimentary to elaborate. The secret to making the delectable Café au Lait Soufflé is beating egg whites at room temperature until they form stiff peaks. Kids may have fun helping with the Princess Fudge Fruitcake with its caramelized Christmas trees. The Shimmering Croquembouche, however, will take a few practice tries for even the experienced chef, but will be well worth the effort.

Above: This pyramid of yummy cream puffs is held together by fine strands of spun sugar. Be sure to serve immediately, because the sugar web will quickly melt. But don't worry—a dessert as lovely and delectable as Shimmering Croquembouche can't help but disappear as quickly as its sugar web.

Opposite: This heavenly Golden White-Chocolate Cake may make appreciative guests suggest a halo for the cook. For information on how to order the chalkware Santa, far right, see source listing on page 154.

Princess Fudge Fruitcake

½ cup minced dried apples
⅓ cup currants
⅓ cup cognac
8 ounces semisweet chocolate morsels
½ cup butter
3 eggs, separated
⅔ cup sugar, divided
⅓ cup finely chopped pecans, toasted
¼ cup all-purpose flour
Spiced Buttercream Frosting (recipe follows)
Caramel Christmas Trees (recipe follows)
Additional finely chopped pecans, toasted

Combine dried apples, currants, and cognac in a small bowl; cover and let stand 2 hours.

Combine chocolate morsels and butter in top of a double boiler; bring water to a boil. Reduce heat to low; cook until chocolate melts. Set aside and cool to room temperature.

Beat egg yolks at medium speed of an electric mixer until thick and lemon colored; gradually add ⅓ cup sugar, beating well. Stir in chocolate mixture, ⅓ cup pecans, and flour. Add apple mixture, stirring gently until well blended. Beat egg whites (at room temperature) at high speed of electric mixer until foamy. Gradually add remaining ⅓ cup sugar, 1 tablespoon at a time, beating until stiff peaks form and sugar dissolves. Gently fold a third of egg whites into chocolate mixture; fold in remaining egg whites.

Grease and flour a 9″ round cakepan; line bottom with wax paper. Pour batter into pan. Bake at 350° for 35 minutes. Cool cake completely in pan on wire rack. Remove from pan; transfer to serving plate.

Reserve ⅓ cup of Spiced Buttercream Frosting; spread remaining frosting on top and sides of cake. Arrange Caramel Christmas Trees on cake, using reserved frosting to secure in place. Sprinkle additional pecans around trees. Serve at room temperature. Yield: one 1-layer cake.

Spiced Buttercream Frosting:

½ cup butter or margarine, softened
1⅓ cups sifted powdered sugar
1½ teaspoons milk
¼ teaspoon ground cinnamon
⅛ teaspoon ground cloves
¼ teaspoon vanilla extract

Cream butter at medium speed of an electric mixer; gradually add sugar, beating until light and fluffy. Add milk, cinnamon, and cloves; beat until spreading consistency. Stir in vanilla. Yield: 1½ cups.

Caramel Christmas Trees:

1 cup sugar

Crumple a large piece of aluminum foil; uncrumple and flatten with your hand, leaving some crumpled detail in foil. Cover a baking sheet with prepared foil, and brush foil lightly with oil.

Coat several 2″ to 3½″ Christmas tree cookie cutters with oil and place on prepared foil; set aside.

Place sugar in a heavy saucepan. Cook over low heat, without stirring, until sugar begins to melt. Increase heat to medium low; cook, stirring constantly, until sugar melts and turns a light golden brown. Remove from heat.

Carefully pour caramelized sugar into each cookie cutter to a ⅛″ thickness. Cool completely. Discard remaining caramelized sugar.

To remove cookie cutters, gently hold center of tree in place with a wooden pick; carefully lift cookie cutters. Yield: 3 to 4 trees.

Café au Lait Soufflé

2 envelopes unflavored gelatin
1 cup cold milk
1 cup sugar, divided
1 cup strong brewed coffee
2 egg whites
2 cups whipping cream, whipped
Sweetened whipped cream
Lace Caramel Fans (recipe follows)
Candied coffee beans (optional)

Cut a piece of aluminum foil long enough to fit around a 1-quart soufflé dish, allowing a 1″ overlap; fold foil lengthwise into thirds. Lightly oil bottom of dish and 1 side of foil. Wrap foil, with oiled side in, around top of dish, allowing foil to extend 3″ above rim to form a collar; secure with string.

Sprinkle gelatin over milk in a medium saucepan; let stand 1 minute. Cook over low heat until gelatin dissolves. Add ¾ cup sugar and coffee; cook over medium heat, stirring constantly, until sugar dissolves. Chill until coffee mixture is consistency of unbeaten egg whites.

Beat egg whites (at room temperature) at high speed of an electric mixer just until foamy. Gradually add remaining ¼ cup sugar, 1 tablespoon at a time, beating until stiff peaks form and sugar dissolves (2 to 4 minutes). Fold egg whites into chilled coffee mixture. Gently fold in whipped cream. Spoon coffee mixture into prepared dish. Cover and chill at least 8 hours.

Remove collar from dish. Garnish with sweetened whipped cream. Top with Lace Caramel Fans. Sprinkle with candied coffee beans, if desired. Serve immediately. Yield: 8 to 10 servings.

Lace Caramel Fans:

1 cup sugar

Line a baking sheet with aluminum foil and lightly coat with oil. Place sugar in a heavy saucepan. Cook over low heat, without stirring, until sugar begins to melt. Increase heat to medium-low; cook, stirring constantly, until sugar melts and turns a light golden brown. Remove from heat. Quickly drizzle syrup into fan shapes on prepared baking sheet. Cool completely. Carefully remove fans from aluminum foil. Yield: 10 to 12 fans.

Shimmering Croquembouche

2 cups whipping cream
½ cup plus 2 tablespoons sifted powdered sugar
1½ teaspoons ground cinnamon
1 cup sour cream
3 recipes Cream Puffs (recipe follows)
Additional powdered sugar
1 cup sugar
¼ cup water
⅛ teaspoon cream of tartar
Fresh evergreen leaves and cranberries

Beat whipping cream until foamy; gradually add powdered sugar and cinnamon, beating until soft peaks form. Fold in sour cream. Chill.

Cut tops off cream puffs; pull out and discard soft dough inside. Fill cream puffs with whipped cream mixture. Replace tops. Sift additional powdered sugar over cream puff tops.

With a layer of filled cream puffs, form a 9″ circular area on a large round serving platter. Carefully layer remaining cream puffs onto first layer, forming a pyramid. (Pyramid should be about 10″ high.)

With wire clippers, remove balloon end of a large wire whisk, leaving only straight wires. (See whisk in Photo 1 on page 109.)

Combine sugar, water, and cream of tartar in a heavy saucepan. Cook over medium heat, without stirring, to hard crack stage (310°). Remove from heat; let syrup cool slightly (about 6 to 8 minutes).

Dip prepared wire whisk into hot syrup; let excess drip back into pan. When syrup begins to thread, move whisk over cream puff pyramid in a smooth, steady motion, working quickly. Repeat procedure until cream puff pyramid is covered with spun sugar. Garnish with evergreen leaves and cranberries. Yield: about 30 servings.

Cream Puffs:

1 cup water
½ cup unsalted butter
2 tablespoons sugar
½ teaspoon vanilla extract
1 cup all-purpose flour
4 eggs
1 egg white, lightly beaten

Combine water, unsalted butter, sugar, and vanilla in a medium saucepan; bring to a boil. Reduce heat to medium; add flour all at once, stirring vigorously 1 minute or until mixture leaves sides of pan and forms a smooth ball. Remove from heat and cool slightly.

Add eggs to flour mixture, one at a time, beating well with a wooden spoon after each addition; beat until batter is smooth. Spoon batter into pastry bag fitted with a ½″ plain tip. Pipe batter into 2″ circles, 3″ apart, on greased baking sheets; lightly brush with beaten egg white. Bake at 400° for 10 minutes; reduce heat to 350° and bake an additional 20 minutes or until lightly browned. Remove from baking sheet and let cool on wire racks. Yield: 1½ dozen.

Spun Sugar Nests with Ice Cream And Date-Nut Topping

2 tablespoons butter or margarine
⅓ cup chopped pecans
1⅓ cups whipping cream
⅓ cup firmly packed brown sugar
⅓ cup dark rum
⅓ cup chopped pitted dates
Spun Sugar Nests (recipe follows)
French vanilla ice cream

Melt butter in a small heavy skillet over medium heat; add pecans. Cook 6 to 8 minutes or until nuts are toasted, stirring frequently. Remove from heat and set aside.

Combine whipping cream, brown sugar, and rum in a small saucepan. Bring to a boil; cook over medium-high heat 5 to 8 minutes or until rum mixture reduces to 1 cup. Stir in toasted pecans and dates.

Place Spun Sugar Nests in serving bowls; scoop ice cream in center of nests and top with Date-Nut Topping. Yield: 6 to 8 servings.

Spun Sugar Nests:

2 cups sugar
½ cup water
¼ teaspoon cream of tartar

Place 2 wooden dowels or wooden spoons on table 10″ to 12″ apart, allowing ends or handles to extend about 10″ beyond edge of table; secure with tape. (Refer to Photo 1 on page 109.) Completely cover floor with wax paper or other disposable protective covering.

With wire clippers, remove balloon end of a large wire whisk, leaving only straight wires. (See whisk in Photo 1 on page 109.)

Combine all ingredients in a heavy saucepan. Cook over medium heat, without stirring, to hard crack stage (310°). Remove from heat; let syrup cool slightly (about 6 to 8 minutes).

Dip prepared wire whisk into hot syrup; let excess drip back into pan. When syrup begins to thread, move whisk back and forth above wooden dowels. When bundle of strands is several inches thick, lift gently. (Refer to Photo 2 on page 109.) Shape strands into nests. Repeat procedure with remaining syrup. Yield: 6 to 8 nests.

Golden White-Chocolate Cake

12 ounces premium white chocolate, coarsely chopped
¼ cup hot water
⅓ cup honey
½ cup butter or margarine, softened
¾ cup sugar
4 eggs
2 cups all-purpose flour
¾ teaspoon baking soda
½ teaspoon salt
¼ teaspoon baking powder
¾ cup sour cream
½ cup chopped hazelnuts
1 teaspoon vanilla extract
White-Chocolate Frosting (recipe follows)
Spun Sugar Halo (recipe follows)
White-chocolate leaves

Combine chocolate and water in top of a double boiler; bring water to a boil. Reduce heat to low; cook until chocolate melts. Stir in honey; set aside and let cool to lukewarm.

Cream butter; gradually add sugar, beating well at medium speed of an electric mixer. Add eggs, one at a time, beating well after each addition. Add chocolate mixture to creamed mixture, beating well.

Combine flour and next 3 ingredients; add to creamed mixture alternately with sour cream, beginning and ending with flour mixture. Mix after each addition. Stir in hazelnuts and vanilla.

Grease and flour 3 (8″) round cakepans, and line with wax paper; grease and flour wax paper. Pour batter into pans. Bake at 350° for 30 minutes or until a wooden pick inserted in center comes out clean. Cool in pans 10 minutes; remove from pans and let cool completely on wire racks. Spread White-Chocolate Frosting between layers and on top and sides of cake. Garnish with Spun Sugar Halo and white-chocolate leaves. Yield: one 3-layer cake.

White-Chocolate Frosting:

12 ounces premium white chocolate, coarsely chopped
1½ cups butter
¾ cup sifted powdered sugar
4 egg whites

Place white chocolate in top of a double boiler; bring water to a boil. Reduce heat to low; cook until chocolate melts. Remove from heat, stir until smooth, and cool to lukewarm.

Cream butter in a large mixing bowl; gradually add sugar, beating until light and fluffy. Add chocolate mixture to creamed mixture, beating well. Add egg whites, one at a time, beating well after each addition. Yield: 4½ cups.

Spun Sugar Halo:

2 cups sugar
½ cup water
¼ teaspoon cream of tartar

Place 2 wooden dowels or wooden spoons on table 10″ to 12″ apart, allowing ends or handles to extend about 10″ beyond edge of table; secure with tape. (Refer to Photo 1, top right.) Completely cover floor with wax paper or other disposable protective covering.

With wire clippers, remove balloon end of a large wire whisk, leaving only straight wires. (See whisk in Photo 1, top right.)

Combine all ingredients in a heavy saucepan. Cook over medium heat, without stirring, to hard crack stage (310°). Remove from heat; let syrup cool slightly (about 6 to 8 minutes).

Dip prepared wire whisk into hot syrup; let excess drip back into pan. When syrup begins to thread, move whisk back and forth above wooden dowels. When bundle of strands is several inches thick, lift gently. (Refer to Photo 2, bottom right.) Shape strands into a 7″ circle. Discard remaining syrup or reserve for other uses. Yield: one 7″ halo.

Photo 1: Dip prepared wire whisk into hot syrup; let excess drip back into pan. When syrup begins to thread, move whisk back and forth above wooden dowels. The strands should be very fine and golden colored.

Photo 2: When bundle of strands is several inches thick, lift gently and shape.

Spun Sugar Suggestions

Years ago, cooks made spun sugar using just a fork to do their spinning or drizzling. The fork works, but it is a slow process, and the syrup may cool and harden before the spinning is finished. The straight wires from the wire whisk will help speed up the spinning process, but you'll still need to work quickly.

It is best not to make spun sugar on a rainy day or during other periods of high humidity. Excessive humidity makes spun sugar sticky and causes it to string improperly. Spun sugar begins to melt after 1 to 2 hours, depending on humidity.

Three important points to remember when making spun sugar are: 1) Be sure to completely cover the floor under the area where you'll be working. 2) Bring the sugar syrup to the correct temperature *slowly*. 3) Cream of tartar is essential; it acts as a stabilizer.

Easygoing Entertaining

In the midst of the holidays, guests always expect to find glorious food. For the hostess, however, there never seems to be enough time to prepare everything. Here are some suggestions to keep entertaining simple, yet luscious.

Left: A dessert classic is only minutes away when you add your personal touch to commercially available cheesecake (found in the freezer section of most large grocery stores). Spread ¾ cup vanilla-flavored ready-to-spread frosting on sides of cheesecake. Cut chocolate wafer cookies in half; press into frosting, allowing wafers to overlap. Top with fresh strawberries for a stunning dessert.

Great Beginnings

♥ Almond-Chicken Stuffed Pastry

Fill commercial 2″ puff pastry patty shells (available in the breads section of grocery stores) with deli chicken salad. Sprinkle the tops with toasted almonds for an appetizer that will taste as if it took you hours to make.

♥ Pesto Spread

Fill a small crock with alternate layers of softened cream cheese and commercial pesto. Serve with toasted pita wedges or bagel chips.

♥ Avocado Beef Rolls

Combine 1 (8-ounce) package softened cream cheese and 1 (8-ounce) container commercial avocado dip; beat at medium speed of an electric mixer until creamy. Spread over 8″ flour tortillas. Top with thinly sliced roast beef and shredded Monterey Jack cheese with jalapeño peppers. Roll up, cut in half or in ½″ pieces, and serve with salsa.

Sweet Endings

♥ Fruit and Spirits

Set out a selection of liqueurs, fruit, and ice cream and let your guests create their own taste-tempting desserts.

They can start with a scoop of ice cream, sorbet, or sherbet in a stemmed glass, spoon on fruit to cover, and then top this with a splash of liqueur. Here are some terrific combinations to get your guests started: chocolate-almond ice cream, sliced peaches, and amaretto; or orange sherbet, fresh orange sections, and Galliano; or buttercrunch ice cream, sliced bananas, and Drambuie.

Opposite: Combine the crunch of cashews with the rich, buttery crumble of shortbread for a quick holiday treat. Dress up purchased shortbread cookies by dipping them in melted caramel or chocolate, and then rolling them in finely chopped cashews.

Above: For a hostess gift with plenty of spice, give several of these individual bouquets garnis. Combine bay leaves, cloves of garlic, dried onion flakes, peppercorns, dried whole thyme, and dried whole marjoram in a small bowl; toss gently. Place two teaspoons herb mixture in the center of five-inch square of cheesecloth. Tie with string and attach a note that describes the uses of bouquets garnis in seasoning soups, stews, and stocks.

Worth Giving

♥ Rice Pilaf Mix

Combine ½ to 1 teaspoon of your choice of dried herbs or spices and 1 cup uncooked instant rice in a decorative jar. Add other ingredients to make your mix interesting, such as dried fruits, dried parsley flakes, toasted chopped nuts, or chicken-flavored bouillon granules. Include directions from package for cooking instant rice.

Above: Because nothing enhances a green salad, vegetables, or meats like freshly ground pepper, a pepper mill filled with a combination of red, white, and green peppercorns makes a speedy gift for the gourmet on your list.

Pleasures of the Season

HOST A HOLIDAY TEA

THE CHRISTMAS TREE

CAROLERS SING FOR
THEIR SUPPER

IDEAS: SURPRISING
PACKAGES

Above: A table laden with tempting delights includes, clockwise from top: English Tea Scones, Whipped Chambord Butter, piped Ginger-Lime Butter, Strawberry Sandwich Cookies, and Cranberry Cordial.

114

Host a Holiday Tea

A cup of steaming hot tea warms the body as good conversation warms the spirit. A holiday gathering over tea, scones, and cookies takes the chill from even the coldest of days.

English Tea Scones

4 cups all-purpose flour
2 tablespoons sugar
1 tablespoon baking powder
¾ teaspoon salt
½ teaspoon baking soda
⅔ cup butter
1¼ cups half-and-half
1 egg, slightly beaten
½ cup raisins (optional)
Additional half-and-half
Additional sugar

Combine first 5 ingredients in a large bowl; stir well. Cut in butter with a pastry blender until mixture resembles coarse meal. Combine 1¼ cups half-and-half, egg, and, if desired, raisins; gradually add to flour mixture, stirring just until dry ingredients are moistened. Turn dough out onto a lightly floured surface and knead lightly 4 to 5 times.

Divide dough in half. Roll each half into an 8″ circle. Transfer to a greased baking sheet. Cut into 8 pie-shaped wedges; separate slightly. Brush scones with additional half-and-half and sprinkle with sugar. Bake at 400° for 16 to 18 minutes or until golden brown. Serve warm or at room temperature with assorted jams or flavored butters. Yield: 16 scones.

Whipped Chambord Butter

1 (10-ounce) package frozen raspberries in
   light syrup, thawed and undrained
1 to 2 tablespoons Chambord or other
   raspberry-flavored liqueur
½ cup butter, softened

Position knife blade in food processor bowl; add raspberries. Top with cover and process until smooth. Strain raspberry puree; discard seeds. Bring raspberry puree to a boil in a small saucepan over medium heat. Cook 20 minutes or until liquid is reduced to ⅓ cup, stirring frequently. Cool slightly and stir in Chambord. Let cool completely.

Cream butter at high speed of an electric mixer until light and fluffy. Add raspberry mixture, ½ teaspoon at a time, beating until well blended and doubled in bulk. Serve with scones or toast. Yield: 1 cup.

Ginger-Lime Butter

½ cup butter, softened
¼ cup sifted powdered sugar
2 tablespoons water
2 tablespoons freshly squeezed lime juice
1 teaspoon minced crystallized ginger
⅛ teaspoon grated lime rind

Cream butter; gradually add sugar, beating at high speed of an electric mixer until fluffy.

Add water and lime juice, ½ teaspoon at a time, beating until well blended and doubled in bulk. Add ginger and lime rind, beating well. Serve at room temperature. Yield: 1 cup.

Whipped Brandied Butter

½ cup butter, softened
¼ cup sifted powdered sugar
2 tablespoons water
2 tablespoons brandy
⅛ teaspoon ground cinnamon
⅛ teaspoon ground nutmeg

Cream butter; gradually add sugar, beating at high speed of an electric mixer until light and fluffy. Add water and brandy, ½ teaspoon at a time, beating until well blended and doubled in bulk. Beat in cinnamon and nutmeg. Serve at room temperature. Yield: 1 cup.

Strawberry Sandwich Cookies

¼ cup plus 2 tablespoons butter
¾ cup firmly packed brown sugar
1 egg
¾ teaspoon vanilla extract
2 cups all-purpose flour
⅛ teaspoon salt
½ cup strawberry jam
Powdered sugar

Cream butter; gradually add brown sugar, beating at medium speed of an electric mixer until light and fluffy. Add egg and vanilla, beating until well blended.

Combine flour and salt; add to creamed mixture, mixing well. Divide dough in half and wrap in wax paper. Chill 1 hour. Roll half of dough to ⅛″ thickness on a lightly floured surface; keep remaining dough chilled until ready to use. Cut with a 2½″ star-shaped cookie cutter. Transfer cookies to lightly greased cookie sheets. Repeat procedure with remaining dough, cutting out center of each cookie in this portion of dough with a 1″ star-shaped cookie cutter. Bake at 350° for 5 to 6 minutes or until lightly browned. Let cool slightly on cookie sheets; remove to wire racks to cool completely.

Spread solid cookies evenly with jam. Dust cookies with cutout centers lightly with powdered sugar. Top solid cookies with sugar-dusted cookies, pressing lightly together to fill cutouts with jam. Yield: about 2½ dozen cookies.

Hot Orange Cream Tea

8 cups boiling water
10 orange-spice herb tea bags
2 cups orange juice
¼ cup honey
Sweetened whipped cream

Pour boiling water over tea bags; cover. Allow tea to steep 10 minutes. Discard tea bags.

Combine tea, orange juice, and honey in a Dutch oven. Keep warm. To serve, fill each tea cup with hot tea and top with a dollop of whipped cream. Serve immediately. Yield: about 10 cups.

Note: In England, tea is usually served with milk or cream. Clotted cream, a dense cream, is used in some regions of England. Whipped cream makes a good American substitute.

Ambassador Turkey Sandwiches

1 (3-ounce) package cream cheese, softened
1 tablespoon apple or pineapple juice
2 tablespoons minced pecans, toasted
1 (8-ounce) can date-nut bread
1 (6-ounce) package thinly sliced turkey
1 medium-size red pear, cored and thinly sliced

Combine cream cheese and juice in a small mixing bowl; beat at high speed of an electric mixer until smooth. Stir in pecans and set aside.

Cut date-nut bread into ¼″ slices; cut each slice in half. Spread cream cheese mixture over each slice of bread. Divide turkey evenly and place on cream cheese mixture. Top with sliced pear. Yield: 20 sandwiches.

Chicken Pâté

1 cup pecan halves, toasted
1 cup walnut halves, toasted
1 pound skinned and boned chicken breast halves, cooked
2 cloves garlic, split
1 cup mayonnaise
2 tablespoons minced crystallized ginger
1 tablespoon soy sauce
1 tablespoon Worcestershire sauce
1 teaspoon lemon juice
½ cup minced green onions
Sour cream
Green onion fans and lemon wedges

Position knife blade in food processor bowl; add pecans and walnuts. Top with cover; process until finely ground. Remove from processor bowl and set aside.

Cut chicken into 1″ cubes. Position knife blade in food processor bowl; add chicken. Top with cover; process until finely ground. Drop garlic through food chute with processor running; process 3 to 5 seconds or until well blended. Add mayonnaise and next 4 ingredients; pulse 3 or 4 times or until well blended. Add nuts and onions; pulse 2 or 3 times or until blended.

Spoon mixture into a 3½-cup mold or two 1½-cup molds; cover and chill at least 8 hours.

Unmold pâté onto a serving platter. Frost with a thin layer of sour cream and garnish with green onion fans and lemon wedges. Yield: 3½ cups.

Below: Offer an alternative to the sweet treats with, top left, Ambassador Turkey Sandwiches topped with red pear slices and a sour-cream frosted Chicken Pâté. Instructions for the Irish Rose Crochet potholders are on page 118.

Gruyère and Spinach Tart

1½ **tablespoons plus 1 teaspoon butter or margarine, melted and divided**
¾ **cup soft French breadcrumbs, toasted**
¼ **pound fresh mushrooms, sliced**
1 **(10-ounce) package frozen chopped spinach, thawed**
2 **(8-ounce) packages cream cheese, softened**
2 **tablespoons milk**
½ **teaspoon salt**
¼ **teaspoon ground nutmeg**
⅛ **teaspoon ground red pepper**
2 **eggs**
¾ **cup (3 ounces) shredded Gruyère cheese**
Fresh spinach leaves and fresh mushrooms (optional)

Combine 1½ tablespoons melted butter and breadcrumbs in a small bowl; stir well. Sprinkle breadcrumb mixture evenly into a well-greased 10″ tart pan, turning the pan to coat both the bottom and the sides. Bake at 350° for 8 minutes or until set.

Sauté mushrooms in remaining 1 teaspoon melted butter in a small skillet until mushrooms are tender. Remove from heat; place on paper towels and pat dry. Set aside.

Drain the spinach; place it on paper towels and squeeze it until it is barely moist. Set the spinach aside.

Combine cream cheese, milk, salt, nutmeg, and red pepper in a medium bowl. Beat at medium-high speed of an electric mixer until smooth; add eggs, one at a time, beating well after each addition.

Divide the cream cheese mixture in half. Add Gruyère cheese and reserved mushrooms to half of the cream cheese mixture. Add the reserved spinach to remaining half of the cream cheese mixture.

Pour spinach mixture into prepared tart pan. Spread Gruyère cheese and mushroom mixture over spinach mixture. Bake at 325° for 40 to 45 minutes or until set.

Cool the tart completely on a wire rack. Serve it at room temperature. Garnish the tart with spinach leaves and mushrooms, if desired. Yield: one 10″ tart.

Chilled Apple Tea Punch

8 cups boiling water
4 lemon herb tea bags
4 cinnamon-apple herb tea bags
2 (12-ounce) cans apple juice concentrate
¼ cup freshly squeezed lemon juice
Ice Ring (recipe follows; optional)

Pour boiling water over tea bags; cover. Allow tea to steep 10 minutes. Discard tea bags.

Combine tea, apple juice concentrate, and lemon juice in large container; stir well. Chill. Serve over ice or in a punch bowl with an ice ring, if desired. Yield: about 9 cups.

Note: This punch is delicious served hot.

Ice Ring:

1 apple, cut into wedges
Lemon juice
2 lemons, sliced
3 cups apple juice

Brush apple wedges with lemon juice; arrange apples and lemon slices in bottom of a 3½-cup ring mold. Add apple juice; freeze until firm. Yield: 1 ice ring.

Cranberry Cordial

10 whole cloves
4 (3½") sticks cinnamon
3 quarts cranberry juice cocktail
2 cups orange juice
¾ cup sugar
4 cups strongly brewed tea
Cinnamon schnapps (optional)
Orange slices (optional)

Combine cloves and cinnamon sticks in a cheesecloth bag. Combine cranberry juice cocktail and orange juice in a large Dutch oven; add spice mixture and bring to a boil. Reduce heat, and simmer 15 minutes. Remove and discard spices; add sugar and tea to juice mixture. Cook over medium heat until thoroughly heated and sugar dissolves. To serve, pour 2 teaspoons schnapps in each cup, if desired. Fill with hot cranberry mixture. Garnish with orange slices, if desired. Serve immediately. Yield: 4 quarts.

Try using these delicate crocheted Irish Rose potholders as decorative touches on your holiday table.

Hexagon Potholder

Materials:
size 10 cotton crochet thread: 1 ball each ecru, red, green
size #7 steel crochet hook (or size to obtain gauge)
1 (½"-diameter) plastic ring

Note: Standard Crochet Abbreviations are on page 153.

GAUGE: 8 dc and 4 rows = 1".

HEXAGON: Make 2. With ecru ch 6, join with a sl st to form a ring. *Rnd 1:* Ch 5 for first dc and ch 2, dc in ring, (ch 2, dc in ring) 4 times, ch 2, sl st to 3rd ch of beg ch-5. *Rnd 2:* Sl st in next ch-2 sp, ch 3 for first dc, (dc, ch 2, 2 dc) in same sp, * ch 1, work a shell of (2 dc, ch 2, 2 dc) in next ch-2 sp, rep from * 4 times more, ch 1, sl st to top of beg ch. *Rnd 3:* Sl st in next dc and ch-2 sp, ch 3 for first dc, (dc, ch 2, 2 dc) in same sp, * ch 1, 2 dc in next ch-1 sp, ch 1, (2 dc, ch 2, 2 dc) in next ch-2 sp, rep from * 4 times more, ch 1, 2 dc in ch-1 sp, ch 1, sl st to top of beg ch. *Rnd 4:* Sl st in next dc and ch-2 sp, ch 3 for first dc, (dc, ch 2, 2 dc) in same sp, * ch 1, dc in next ch-1 sp, dc in each of next 2 dc, dc in next ch-1 sp, ch 1 **, (2 dc, ch 2, 2 dc) in next ch-2 sp, rep from * 5 times more, end last rep at **, sl st to top of beg ch. *Rnds 5-10:* Sl st in next dc and ch-2 sp, ch 3 for first dc, (dc, ch 2, 2 dc) in same sp, * ch 1, dc in ch-1 sp, dc in each dc to next ch-1 sp, dc in ch-1 sp, ch 1 **, (2 dc, ch 2, 2 dc) in next ch-2 sp, rep from * 5 times more, end last rep at **, sl st to top of beg ch. Fasten off after rnd 10.

ASSEMBLY: With wrong sides facing and working through both thicknesses, join red with sl st in ch-1 sp before shell. *Rnd 1:* * Sc in ch-1 sp, ch 3, sc in ch-2 sp of shell, ch 3, sc in ch-1 sp, (ch 3, sk 2 dc, sc between next 2 dc) to next ch-1 sp before shell, rep from * around. Fasten off. *Rnd 2:* Join green with sl st in any ch-3 lp, sc in same lp, (ch 3, sc in next ch-3 lp) around. Fasten off.

FLOWER: With red, ch 6, join with a sl st to form a ring. *Rnd 1:* (Ch 4, sc in ring) 4 times. *Rnd 2:* Work * (sc, 4 hdc, sc) in next ch-4 sp, rep from * 3 times more (4 petals completed). *Rnd 3:* Holding petals to front of work and working in beg ch-6 ring, sl st to place in center of next petal (this makes petals overlap), (ch 4, sc in beg ch-6 ring) 4 times. *Rnd 4:* Work * (sc, 6 hdc, sc) in next ch-4 sp, rep from * 3 times more. *Rnd 5:* Holding petals to front of work and working in beg ch-6 ring, sl st to place in center of next petal, (ch 4, sc in beg ch-6 ring) 4 times. *Rnd 6:* Work * (sc, 2 hdc, 5 dc, 2 hdc, sc) in next ch-4 sp, rep from * 3 times more. Fasten off. *Rnd 7:* Join green with sl st in beg ch-6 ring of flower. Holding petals to front of work, (ch 6, sc in ch-6 ring of flower) 5 times, ch 6, sl st in same place as joining. *Rnd 8:* Sl st in ch-6 lp, ch 3 for first dc, 3 dc in same lp, ch 11, sl st in first ch of ch-11, 4 dc in same lp, * (4 dc, ch 11, sl st in first ch of ch-11, 4 dc) in next ch-6 lp, rep from * 4 times more, sl st to top of beg ch-3. Fasten off.

FINISHING: With red, work sc sts around plastic ring until it is completely covered. Fasten off. Attach ring to edging at point directly above ch-2 sp of any shell.

Center flower on potholder with ch-11 lps matched to ch-2 sps of shells. Tack center of each ch-11 lp in place. Weave in all ends.

Square Potholder

Materials:
size 10 cotton crochet thread: 1 ball each red, green, ecru
size #7 steel crochet hook (or size to obtain gauge)
1 (½″-diameter) plastic ring

Note: Standard Crochet Abbreviations are on page 153.
GAUGE: 8 dc and 4 rows = 1″.
FLOWER: With red, ch 8, join with a sl st to form a ring. *Rnd 1:* (Ch 3, sl st in ring) 8 times. *Rnd 2:* (Sl st, 3 sc, sl st) in each lp around. *Rnd 3:* (Ch 4, sl st between next 2 petals) 8 times. *Rnd 4:* (Sc, 5 hdc, sc) in each lp around, sl st to first sc. *Rnd 5:* (Ch 5, sl st between next 2 petals) 8 times. *Rnd 6:* (Sc, 9 hdc, sc) in each lp around, sl st to first sc. *Rnd 7:* (Ch 6, sl st between next 2 petals) 8 times. *Rnd 8:* (Sc, 11 hdc, sc) in each lp around, sl st to first sc. Fasten off.

LEAVES: Join green with sl st to center st of any petal. * (Ch 4, hdc in 3rd ch from hook, ch 3, sl st in first ch of beg ch-4) 3 times, fasten off. Sk next petal, join green with sl st to center st of next petal, rep from * 3 times more.

SQUARE: Join ecru with sl st to center st of any petal between leaf clusters. *Rnd 1:* Ch 8 for first dc and ch 5, * (sc in tip of next leaf, ch 3) twice, sc in tip of next leaf, ch 5 **, dc in center st of next petal, ch 5, rep from * 3 times more, end last rep at **, sl st to 3rd ch of beg ch-8. *Rnd 2:* Ch 4 for first dc and ch 1, sk 1 st, * (dc in next st, ch 1, sk 1 st) to next corner, work a corner shell of (3 dc, ch 2, 3 dc) in sc at tip of center leaf, ch 1, sk 1 st, rep from * around, end with sl st in 3rd ch of beg ch-4. *Rnds 3-6:* Ch 4 for first dc and ch 1, * (dc in next dc, ch 1) to corner shell, dc in first dc of corner shell, ch 1, sk 2 dc, (3 dc, ch 2, 3 dc) in corner ch-2 sp, ch 1, sk 2 dc, dc in last dc of corner shell, ch 1, rep from * around, end with sl st in 3rd ch of beg ch. Fasten off after rnd 6.

BACK: With ecru, ch 44, turn. *Row 1:* Dc in 4th ch from hook and in each ch across. Ch 3, turn. *Rows 2-19:* Dc in each dc across row, ch 3, turn. Fasten off after row 19.

ASSEMBLY: With wrong sides facing and working through both thicknesses, join ecru with sl st in any corner sp. *Rnd 1:* Sc in same corner, * ch 3, sk 3 dc, sc in next sp, (ch 3, sk dc, ch-1 sp, and dc, sc in next sp) to next corner shell, ch 3, sk 3 dc, sc in corner sp, rep from * around, end with sl st in first sc. Fasten off. *Rnd 2:* Join red with sl st in any ch-3 lp, (2 sc, ch 1, 2 sc) in each ch-3 lp around. Fasten off.

FINISHING: With red, work sc sts around plastic ring until it is completely covered. Fasten off. Attach ring to any corner.

Above: The Boehlke farm, where the Sterns choose a tree each year, is named Lovers Lane. The Boehlkes started planting trees on their 20 acres in 1958, because they "wanted green in winter." Now, Austrian pine, Scotch pine, white pine, Black Hills spruce, and Colorado blue spruce guard pathways through the property. Some trees stand 30 feet high.

Above: Al's grandfather used these red runners on his sleigh to help him haul milk to the cheese factories. Al built a new sleigh body so that it could carry more riders safely.

The Christmas Tree

A simple evergreen can give some of the most memorable and significant Christmas joys. The fresh green tree in stark winter signifies everlasting life and the hope of spring to come.

In many families, every step in choosing this centerpiece of the Christmas spirit is a tradition. Excitement builds as the family makes plans in a busy holiday schedule to gather for the annual tree-cutting excursion.

Some families must have a short-needled pine. Other families choose a balsam fir that fills the room with the scent of sweet evergreen. And for still other families, disagreement has become the tradition when choosing a tree.

Not for the Stern family of Arbor Wind Farms near Cedarburg, Wisconsin.

"Most of the time we're on the same wavelength," Cathy Stern says. "We always have a Scotch pine, with its medium-length needles. They let our antique ornaments hang so nicely. We put the tree in the front room where the ceiling is eight feet high. And we know the tree must have room at the top for our porcelain angel."

Cathy and her husband, Al, have a sideline business made for the Christmas season. Thanks to a pair of 2,000-pound Belgian draft horses, they offer sleigh rides, hayrides, and carriage rides all around the Cedarburg area. And on the first weekend in December, Cathy and Al, with their children, Allen and Catrina, take time to choose a tree from a neighbor's tree farm.

"What makes it so wonderful is that we're all together," Cathy says. "It's just been a tradition for as long as I can remember. My gramma and grandpa always took everyone along. Getting the Christmas tree seems to be just as important as the presents."

Left: The sound of sleigh bells makes a ride unforgettable. The horse on the left wears an eight-foot string of hand-cast brass sleigh bells that Al gave Cathy for Christmas one year.

Carolers Sing for Their Supper

According to custom, strolling carolers should be rewarded along their route with a tasty treat. A hot drink will warm the singers and send them happily on their way. Or you might invite them to come back when they've finished caroling. They'll soon forget their chilled fingers, toes, and noses as they enjoy the delicious feast you've prepared for them.

Begin with Black-Eyed Pea Salsa and Toasted Nut Cracker Bread. Serve coleslaw or salad with Andouille Sausage Stew. Top off the meal with spicy cornbread or tasty popovers. You can count on requests for an encore!

Hot Candy Cane

6 cups milk, divided
8 (1.5-ounce) chocolate-covered peppermint patties, divided
1 cup white crème de cacao, divided (optional)
French vanilla ice cream
Peppermint sticks

Pour 3 cups milk into a small saucepan; cook over medium heat until heated. (Do not boil.) Pour hot milk into blender. Add 4 peppermint patties; top with cover and process until smooth. Add ½ cup crème de cacao, if desired. Pour into mugs. Top with scoop of ice cream. Garnish with peppermint sticks. Repeat procedure with remaining ingredients. Yield: 6 cups.

Milk Chocolate Cream

1½ cups Bailey's Irish Cream
1½ cups Kahlúa or other coffee-flavored liqueur
6 cups chocolate milk
3 cups half-and-half
Sweetened whipped cream
Grated milk chocolate

Combine Irish Cream and Kahlúa. Pour ¼ cup liqueur mixture into each of 12 mugs; set aside.
Combine chocolate milk and half-and-half in a medium saucepan; bring just to a boil over medium heat. Pour hot mixture into mugs. Top with a dollop of sweetened whipped cream. Garnish with grated chocolate. Yield: 12 servings.

Coconut Cream Coffee

6 cups strong brewed coffee, divided
2 cups marshmallow creme, divided
½ cup cream of coconut, divided
½ cup sweetened condensed milk, divided
Additional marshmallow creme (optional)
Sliced almonds, toasted (optional)

Left: These carolers are in for a warming treat—cups of Hot Candy Cane. Peppermint patties and peppermint sticks provide the candy-cane flavor, and French vanilla ice cream adds richness.

Combine half of first 4 ingredients in the container of an electric blender; top with cover and process 10 to 15 seconds or until well blended and frothy. Pour coffee mixture into mugs. Garnish with a dollop of marshmallow creme and almonds, if desired. Repeat procedure with remaining ingredients. Serve immediately. Yield: 8 to 10 servings.

Toasted Nut Cracker Bread

2 packages dry yeast
2 cups warm water (105° to 115°)
⅓ cup firmly packed brown sugar
2 tablespoons shortening
1 tablespoon salt
3 to 3½ cups all-purpose flour, divided
2 cups whole wheat flour
1 cup finely chopped walnuts, toasted

Dissolve yeast in warm water in a large bowl; let stand 5 minutes. Add sugar, shortening, and salt; beat at medium speed of an electric mixer until well blended. Gradually stir in 1½ cups all-purpose flour, whole wheat flour, and nuts. Add enough of remaining all-purpose flour to make a soft dough.

Turn dough out onto a well-floured surface and knead until smooth and elastic (about 5 minutes). Place in a well-greased bowl, turning to grease top. Cover and let rise in a warm place (85°), free from drafts, 1 hour or until doubled in bulk.

Punch dough down and divide into 18 portions; let rest 5 minutes. Roll each portion into an 8″ (⅛″-thick) circle and place on a greased baking sheet. Let rest 5 minutes. Bake at 400° for 8 to 10 minutes or until lightly browned. Let cool on wire racks. Serve with Black-Eyed Pea Salsa. Yield: 1½ dozen.

Black-Eyed Pea Salsa

1 (15½-ounce) can black-eyed peas, drained
2 large tomatoes, chopped or 1 (16-ounce) can plum tomatoes, drained and coarsely chopped
1 (4-ounce) can chopped green chilies
2 green onions, chopped
2 canned jalapeño peppers, seeded and chopped
3 tablespoons olive oil
1 tablespoon white wine vinegar
1 clove garlic, minced
½ teaspoon salt
¼ teaspoon pepper
Green onion fans

Combine peas, tomatoes, chilies, onions, peppers, olive oil, vinegar, garlic, salt, and pepper in a medium bowl; stir well. Cover and chill at least 8 hours. Garnish with green onion fans. Serve with Toasted Nut Cracker Bread. Yield: about 2 cups.

Green and Red Pepper Coleslaw

½ small cabbage, thinly sliced (about 5½ cups)
2 small green peppers, cut into julienne strips
½ (15½-ounce) jar roasted red peppers, drained and cut into julienne strips
½ cup thinly sliced sweet pickles
¼ cup vegetable oil
3 tablespoons sugar
3 tablespoons white wine vinegar
½ teaspoon salt
½ teaspoon celery seeds
¼ teaspoon pepper

Combine cabbage, peppers, and pickles in a large bowl; toss gently. Combine vegetable oil, sugar, white wine vinegar, and salt in a small bowl; stir well and pour over cabbage mixture.
Chill at least 8 hours. Yield: 12 to 14 servings.

Bacon and Green Chili Cornbread

8 slices bacon
½ cup chopped green onions
2 cups self-rising cornmeal
½ teaspoon salt
½ teaspoon garlic powder
1¼ cups plus 2 tablespoons buttermilk
2 eggs, slightly beaten
1 (4-ounce) can chopped green chilies, undrained
1 tablespoon shortening

Cook bacon until crisp in a 10″ cast-iron skillet; reserve 2 tablespoons drippings. Crumble bacon and set aside. Sauté onions in reserved drippings in cast-iron skillet until tender. Remove from skillet and set aside.
Combine cornmeal, salt, and garlic powder in a medium bowl. Add buttermilk and eggs; stir well. Stir in reserved bacon, sautéed onions, and chilies. Place shortening in same skillet. Heat skillet in oven at 400° for 4 to 5 minutes or until thoroughly heated. Remove from oven; spoon batter into skillet. Bake at 400° for 25 minutes or until golden brown. Serve hot. Yield: 12 servings.

A Silent Night

Although Michael Haydn has been given credit for composing "Silent Night," folklore says otherwise. More than 100 years ago in Arnsdorf, Austria, Father Josef Mohr was deeply troubled because mice had eaten away the organ bellows, and there would be no organ music for Christmas Eve midnight Mass.

The night before Christmas Eve, Father Mohr was walking home from administering last rites to a parishioner. On this snowy evening, he was touched by the vast stillness and thought how the night of Christ's birth must have been much the same. He hurried home and, before the night was over, had composed one of the most beautiful and enduring of Christmas carols.

Arising the next morning, Father Mohr reread his manuscript and hastened to show it to his organist and friend, Franz Gruber. Father Mohr and Franz sang the holy carol to an enthralled congregation on Christmas Eve, accompanied only by Franz's guitar.

Red Broccoli Salad

3 cups thinly sliced red cabbage
3 cups broccoli flowerets
½ cup golden raisins
¾ cup commercial ranch salad dressing
½ cup sour cream
2 tablespoons sugar
2 tablespoons white wine vinegar

Combine cabbage, broccoli, and raisins in a large bowl; toss gently. Combine salad dressing and remaining ingredients in a small bowl; stir well and add to broccoli mixture, tossing until well blended. Cover and chill up to 1 hour. Yield: 12 servings.

Andouille Sausage Stew

3 tablespoons bacon drippings
2 cups finely chopped onions, divided
1¾ cups chopped celery
1½ cups finely chopped green pepper
¼ cup butter or margarine
3 cloves garlic, minced
2½ cups chicken broth, divided
1 tablespoon dried whole thyme
1½ teaspoons salt
1½ teaspoons dried whole basil
¾ teaspoon ground white pepper
¾ teaspoon pepper
¼ teaspoon ground red pepper
1 bay leaf
3 cups finely chopped peeled tomatoes
1 (15-ounce) can tomato sauce
2 pounds Andouille sausage, cut diagonally
  into ½"-thick slices
1 tablespoon sugar

Heat bacon drippings in a large Dutch oven over medium heat until hot. Add 1 cup onions; cook over high heat 3 minutes, stirring frequently. Reduce heat to medium-low; cook until onions are caramel in color, about 3 to 5 minutes.

Add remaining onions, celery, green pepper, butter, and garlic. Cook until celery is tender. Stir in 1 cup chicken broth and next 7 ingredients. Cook, uncovered, over medium heat 5 minutes, stirring frequently. Stir in tomato; cover and simmer 10 minutes, stirring frequently. Add remaining 1½ cups chicken broth, tomato sauce, sausage, and sugar; stir well. Cover and simmer 15 minutes or until thick, stirring occasionally. Remove and discard bay leaf.

Let cool to room temperature; chill up to 24 hours. Remove and discard fat, if desired. Serve hot with Bacon and Green Chili Cornbread. Yield: 13 cups.

Bacon Popovers

3 slices bacon
1 cup all-purpose flour
2 tablespoons grated Parmesan cheese
¼ teaspoon salt
1 cup milk
2 eggs, slightly beaten

Cook bacon until crisp; crumble and set aside. Reserve drippings.

Combine bacon and remaining ingredients in a medium bowl; beat at low speed of an electric mixer just until smooth.

Grease muffin pans with reserved bacon drippings. Place in a 425° oven for 3 minutes or until a drop of water sizzles when dropped in grease. Remove pans from oven; fill half full of batter. Bake at 425° for 15 minutes. Reduce heat to 350° and bake an additional 18 to 20 minutes or until golden brown. Serve immediately. Yield: 1 dozen.

The Caroling Tradition

Originally a ring dance celebrating winter solstice, the carol was associated with pagan feasts. Many historians believe that St. Francis of Assisi was the first to give the carol Christian significance. It is said that he first adapted carols for use in a Christmas Eve midnight Mass early in the 13th century by replacing pagan lyrics with sacred revisions. In fact, St. Francis was so filled with joy on the occasion that he burst spontaneously into song himself.

Ideas

Surprising Packages

Surprises are at the heart of Christmas. These intriguing packages and wrappings will prolong the suspense and set the stage for the excitement to come.

Above: This beginner's set of Lincoln Logs makes a toy house to be enjoyed long after the sweets are gone. Follow manufacturer's instructions to construct and hot-glue to make the structure permanent. (So that slatted roof can be lifted off, do not glue it to house.) To make a floor, cut mat board to fit bottom and hot-glue to house.

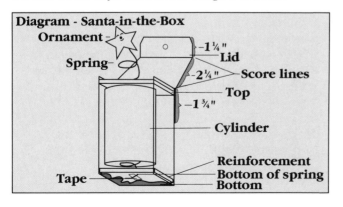

Diagram - Santa-in-the-Box
Ornament
Spring
—1¼"
Lid
—2¼"— Score lines
Top
—1¾"
Cylinder
Reinforcement
Bottom of spring
Tape
Bottom

Santa-in-the-Box

For a real surprise, make a hiding place for a special Santa. The secret to making him work is selecting a low-tension interior spring that is slightly smaller than the cardboard cylinder into which the spring will fit. You'll need a 2¼" x 2¼" x 3" box of heavy cardboard or foam core; 1⅞" square of heavy cardboard for top; cardboard cylinder to fit in box; 5" very low-tension interior spring; 2¼" square of heavy cardboard to reinforce bottom; duct tape or other heavy tape; hot-glue gun with glue sticks; 2¼" x 5¼" piece of heavy cardboard for lid; 2" wooden Santa ornament; scraps of ribbon; wrapping paper; spray glue; 2" (¼"-diameter) wooden dowel; wooden bead to fit dowel.

Note: Follow Diagram to assemble.

In center of cardboard top, cut a round hole slightly smaller than the cardboard cylinder. Cut bottom from box and set aside.

Insert cardboard cylinder into box through bottom and push spring into the cylinder. Push end of spring through center of heavy reinforcement cardboard and tape securely to cutout bottom of box. Then hot-glue both box bottoms and top in place.

Measure 1¾" up from back of box lid and score to bend. Hot-glue this 1¾" portion of lid to back of box. Pull lid over top of box and score 1¼" from top end so that lid will fold over front edge of box. (Remaining 2¼" will cover top of box.) Cut corners from front of box lid at a diagonal. Punch a hole to fit dowel at front edge of lid and a corresponding hole on front of box. (Make sure fit is *very* snug.) Tape ribbon scraps and top end of spring securely to the back of Santa ornament.

Cut the wrapping paper to fit box, lid, and top. Glue the wrapping paper to box, lid, and top with spray glue.

Push the Santa ornament and the spring down into the cardboard cylinder and hold the lid in place with the dowel.

Above: Turn family photographs into unique wrapping paper. Have your favorite color shots photocopied at a print shop and use spray glue to affix to a box. You can use one photo for each side of the box or make a montage.

Above: Here's a different way to stuff a stocking. Tie tiny toys and candies every few inches along a length of colorful yarn. Stuff into a stocking. Add a note (from Santa, of course) to "pull slowly" and watch a little one's eyes light up as he or she reels in the surprises.

Left: This clever magic game will send your child on an exciting gift search. Make a house shape by folding an eight-inch-square piece of paper diagonally in half and then in half again. Trace house pattern (found on page 146) on folded square and cut out. Open house and write a clue with a matchstick and lemon juice. Let dry and refold to house shape. Write "Clue 1" and instructions on this mystery house. Repeat for as many clues as desired. (Note: You will want to supervise this game carefully, since a lighted candle is involved. To reveal the clues, open the house, hold it several inches from a candle, and allow the child to watch the clue magically appear.)

127

Patterns

Precious Angels

Instructions are on page 26.
Patterns are full-size.

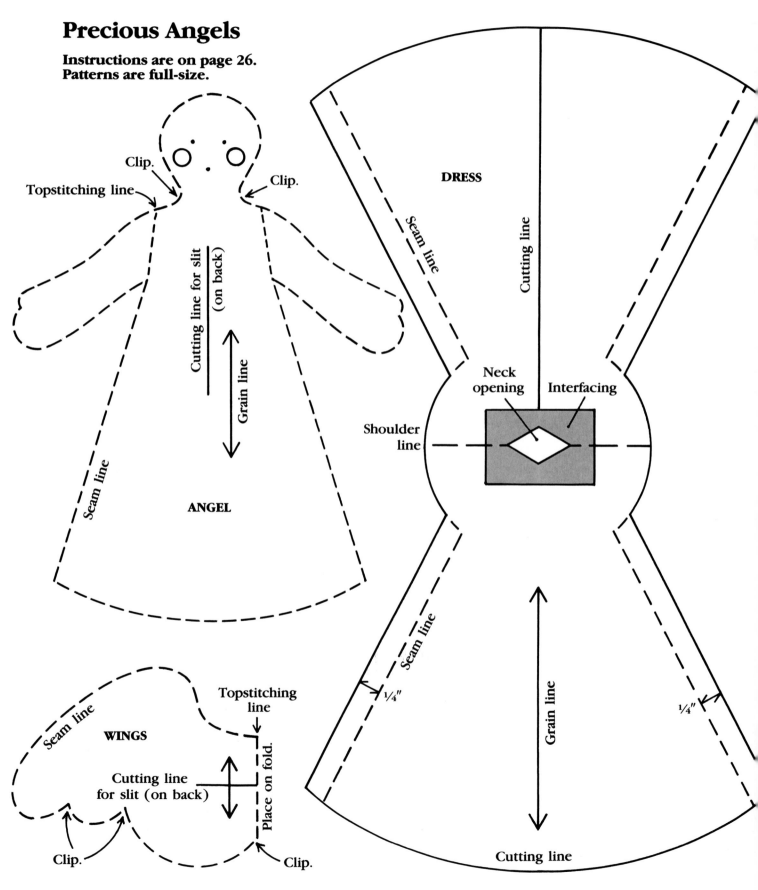

Clip.

Topstitching line

Clip.

Cutting line for slit (on back)

Grain line

Seam line

ANGEL

DRESS

Seam line

Cutting line

Neck opening

Interfacing

Shoulder line

Seam line

¼"

¼"

Grain line

Cutting line

Seam line

Topstitching line

WINGS

Cutting line for slit (on back)

Place on fold.

Clip.

Clip.

Block-Print Cards

**Instructions are on page 54.
Patterns are full-size.**

Color Key
1 Red
2 Green
3 Gold
4 White
5 Black

Relief

Recess

Relief

129

Coverlet Stocking

Instructions are on page 48.
Pattern and chart for stocking

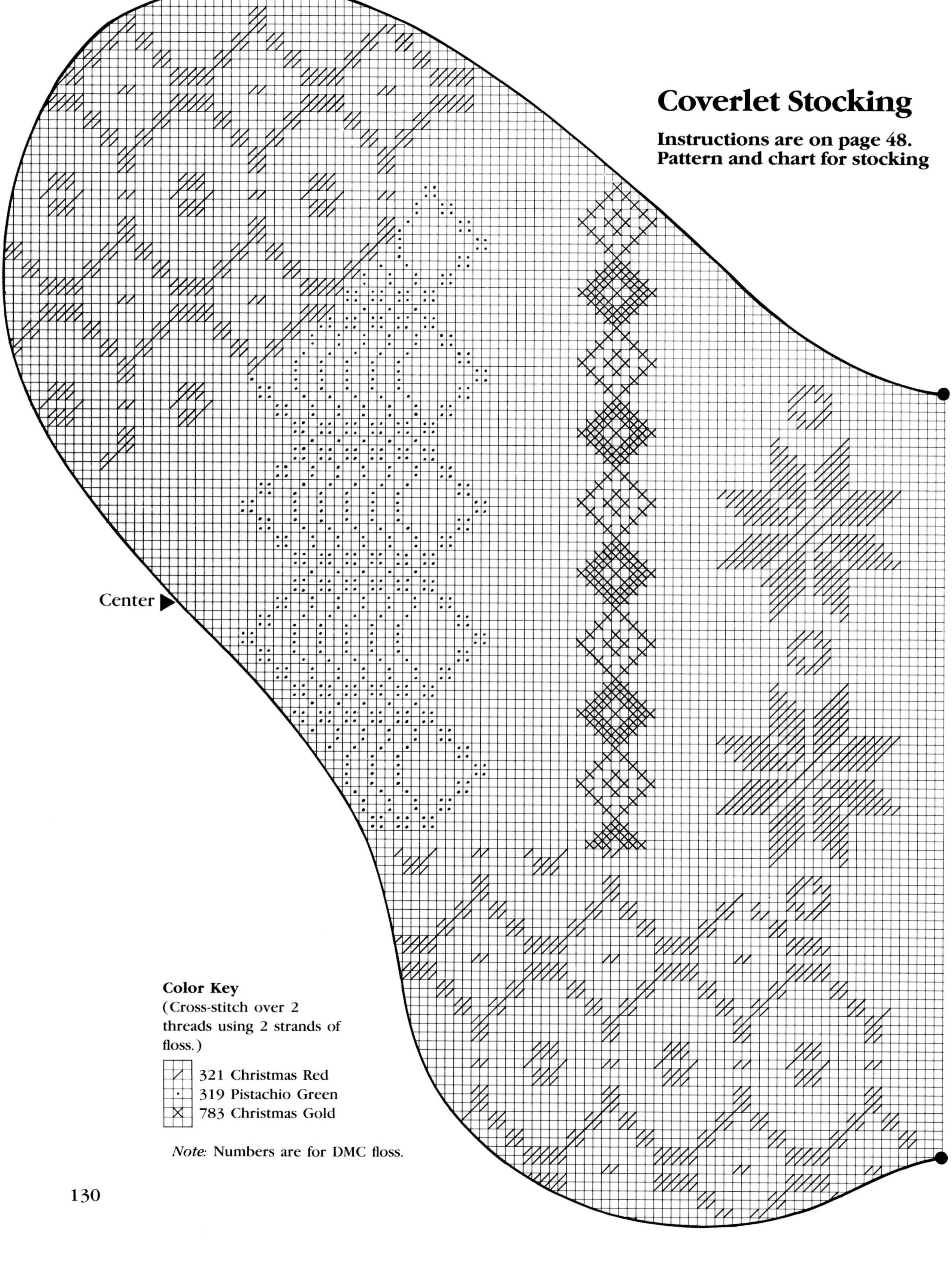

Center ▶

Color Key
(Cross-stitch over 2
threads using 2 strands of
floss.)

/ 321 Christmas Red
· 319 Pistachio Green
✕ 783 Christmas Gold

Note: Numbers are for DMC floss.

Match dots and continue pattern at bottom of next page.

130

Stocking cuff to be worked on wrong side of fabric.

½"

Fold to front here.

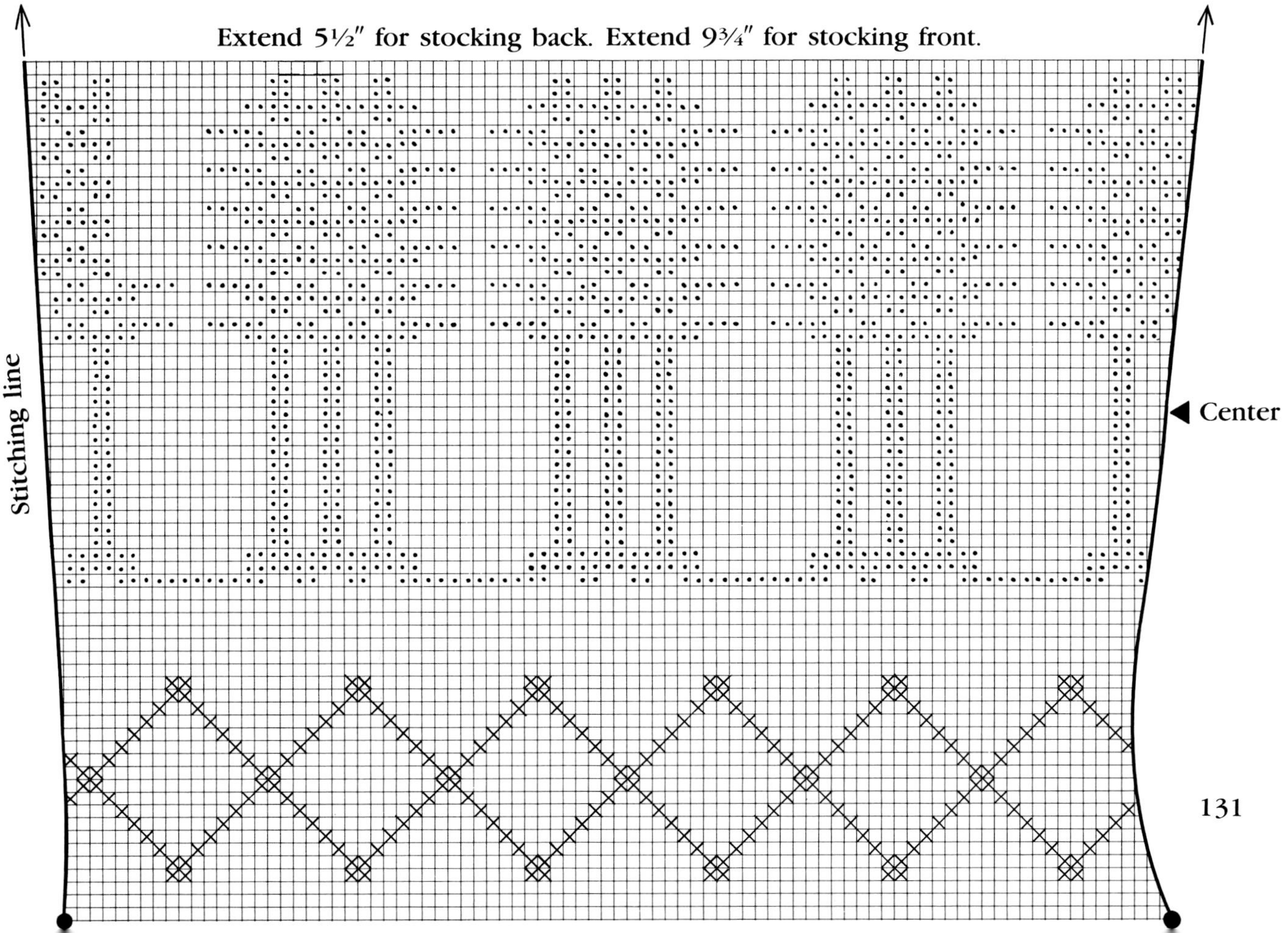

Extend 5½" for stocking back. Extend 9¾" for stocking front.

Stitching line

◄ Center

131

Roly-Poly Santa

Instructions are on page 46.
Pattern is full-size.
All seam allowances are ¼".

HAT BAND
Cut 1 from polar fleece.

Place on fold.

COLLAR
Cut 1 from polar fleece.

Gather.

HAND
Cut 2 from muslin.

Seam line

Leave open.

HAT
Cut 2 from red plaid.

Gather.

BODY
Cut 1 from red plaid.

Place on fold.

Gather.

HEAD
Cut 1 from muslin.

Place on fold.

SANTA BEARD
Cut 1 from crepe-wool hair.

Embossed Cards

**Instructions are on page 54.
Patterns are full-size.**

Seam line

SANTA SLEEVE
Cut 2 from red plaid.

Fold.

Seam line

REINDEER

Tin Stars

**Instructions are on
page 27.
Patterns
are full-size.**

Hole for hanger

Hole for hanger

LARGE STAR

SMALL STAR

CHRISTMAS TREE

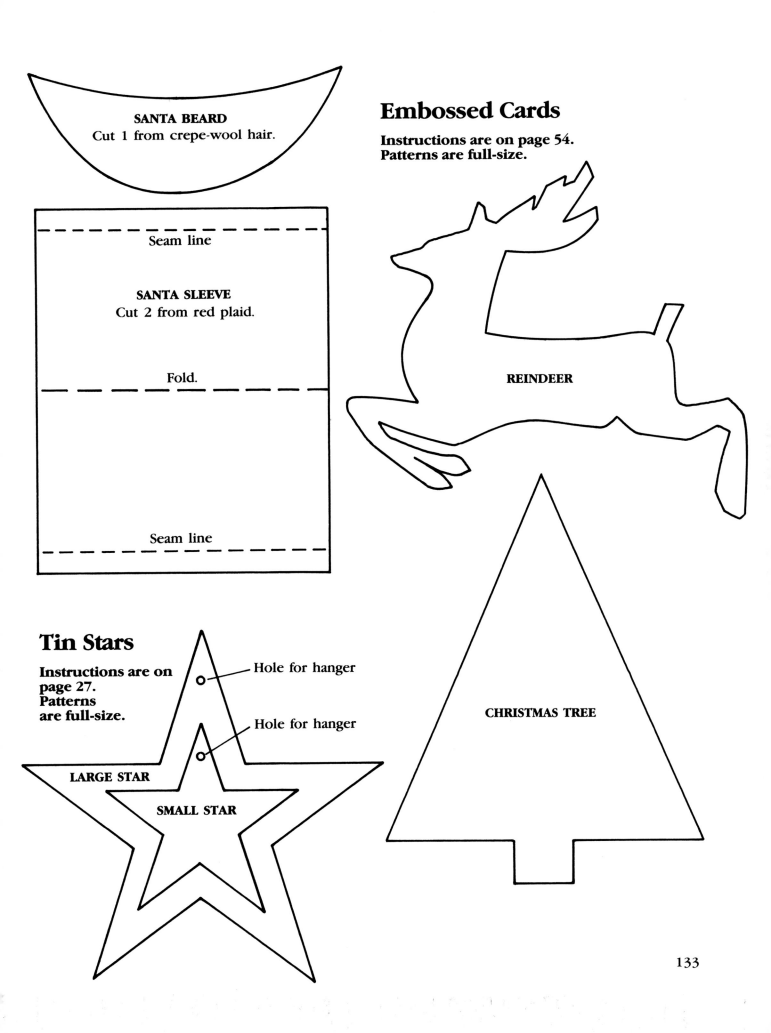

Dancing Children Pillow Cover and Tree Skirt

Instructions are on pages 37, 38. Pattern is full-size.

Placement diagram for finished tree skirt

Match dots and continue pattern across page.

Center of embroidery pattern

134

135

Painted Pillows

Instructions are on page 32.
Patterns are full-size.

Instructions are on page 32.

¼ **BORDER PATTERN**

136

¼ BORDER PATTERN

Color Key

1 Red
2 Light green
3 Medium green
4 Dark green
5 Light blue
6 Medium blue
7 Black
8 Tan
9 Pink
10 Yellow
11 Orange
12 Gold

Note: Use white acrylic for snowflakes and shading on holly berries.

137

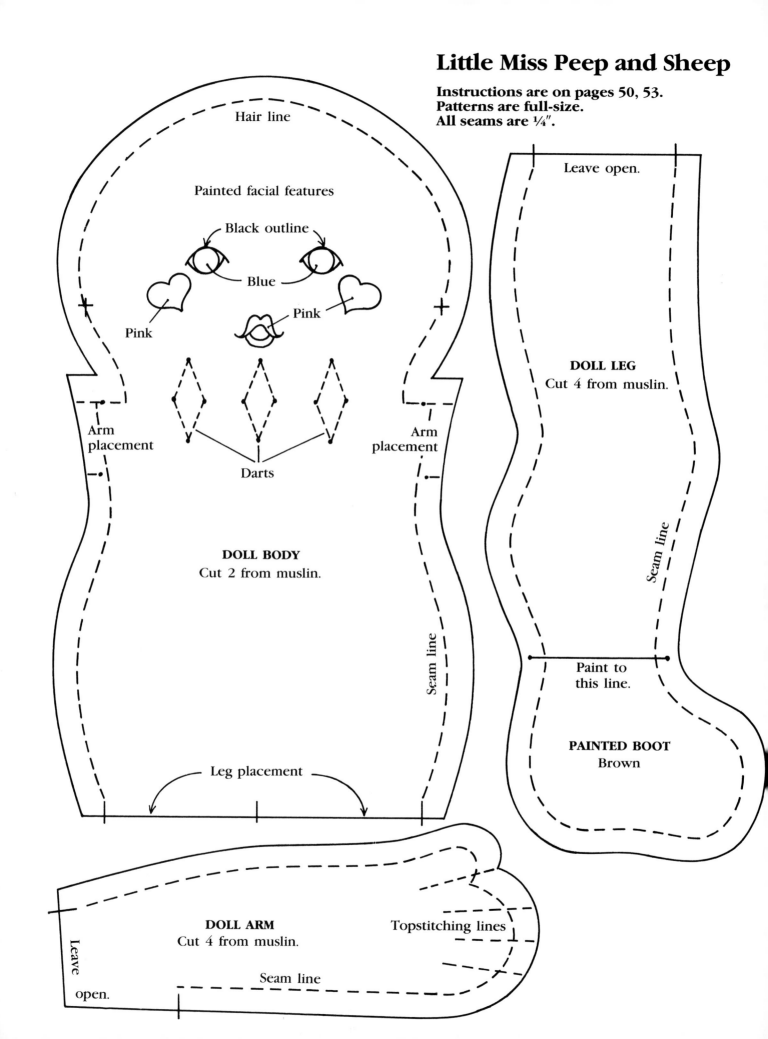

Little Miss Peep and Sheep

Instructions are on pages 50, 53.
Patterns are full-size.
All seams are ¼".

Hair line

Painted facial features

Black outline

Blue

Pink

Pink

Pink

Darts

Arm placement

Arm placement

DOLL BODY
Cut 2 from muslin.

Seam line

Leg placement

Leave open.

DOLL LEG
Cut 4 from muslin.

Seam line

Paint to this line.

PAINTED BOOT
Brown

Leave open.

DOLL ARM
Cut 4 from muslin.

Topstitching lines

Seam line

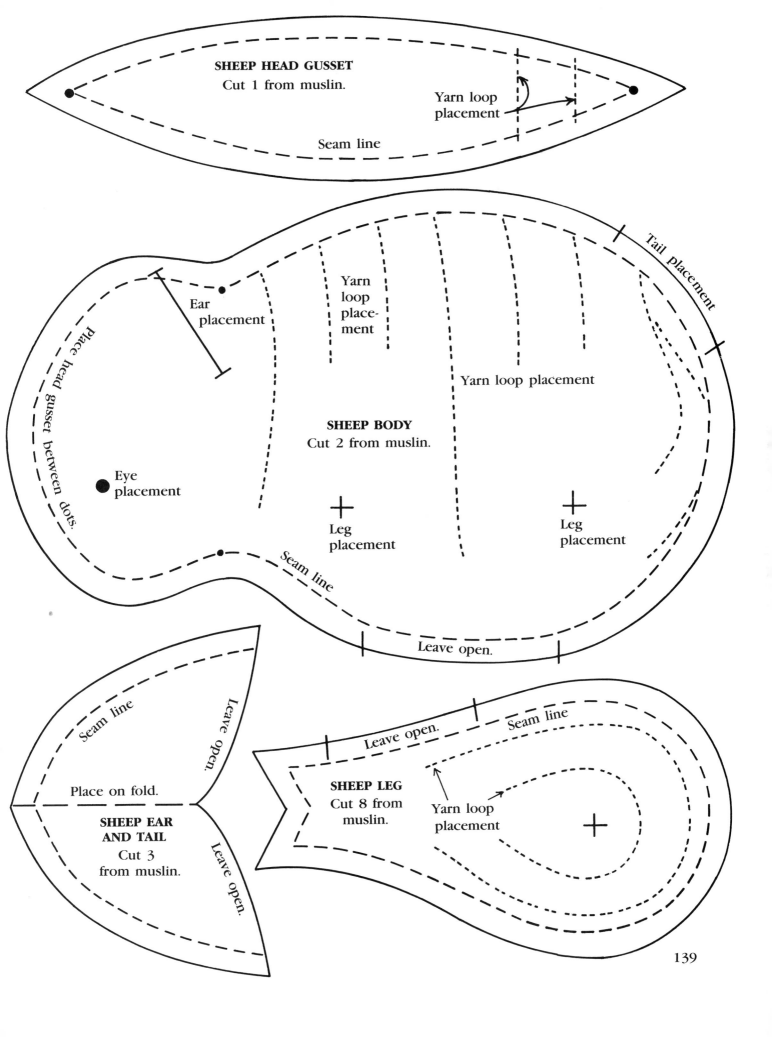

SHEEP HEAD GUSSET
Cut 1 from muslin.

Yarn loop placement

Seam line

Place head gusset between dots.

Ear placement

Yarn loop place- ment

Yarn loop placement

Tail placement

SHEEP BODY
Cut 2 from muslin.

Eye placement

Leg placement

Leg placement

Seam line

Leave open.

Seam line

Leave open.

Place on fold.

Leave open.

SHEEP EAR AND TAIL
Cut 3 from muslin.

Leave open.

Leave open.

Seam line

SHEEP LEG
Cut 8 from muslin.

Yarn loop placement

139

Letter-Perfect Cross-Stitchery

Instructions are on page 42.

Note: In order for colors to show up against cream background, some colors have been changed for pillow. This is indicated on Color Key next to each change. Numbers are for DMC floss.

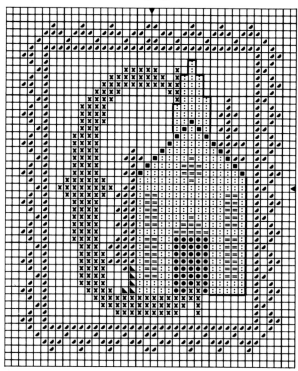

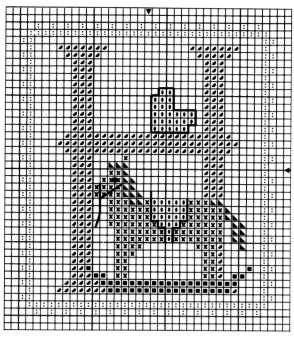

Step 1: Cross-stitch
(2 strands)

=	317 Gray
:	746 Off White
•	801 Brown
X	869 Dk. Tan
◣	898 Dk. Brown
◢	3051 Green
■	3371 Black Brown

Step 2: Backstitch
(2 strands)
317 Gray (steeple,
right side)

Step 1: Cross-stitch
(2 strands)

◆	356 Old Red
:	746 Off White
X	869 Dk. Tan
◣	898 Dk. Brown
◢	3051 Green
■	3371 Black Brown

Step 2: Backstitch
(2 strands)
918 Brick Red (heart)
3371 Black Brown
(saddle, bridle)

Step 3: French Knot
(2 strands)
3371 Black Brown (eye)

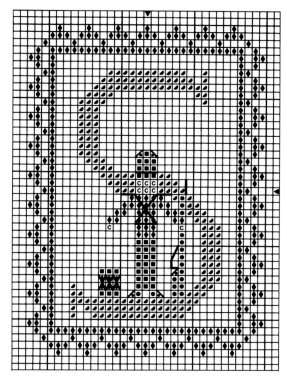

Step 1: Cross-stitch
(2 strands)

C	754 Peach
•	801 Brown
◆	918 Brick Red
◢	3051 Green
■	3371 Black Brown

Step 2: Backstitch
(2 strands)
801 Brown (gun handle,
bayonet)
3046 Lt. Tan (trim on hat,
epaulet, belt)

Step 3: Straight Stitch
(2 strands)
3046 Lt. Tan (drum
strings, 1 strand; chest
straps, 2 strands)

140

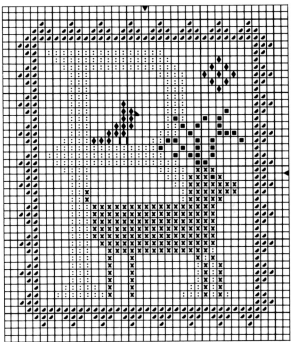

Step 1: Cross-stitch
(2 strands)
746 Off White *OR*
    869 Dk. Tan (for
    pillow)
⊠ 869 Dk. Tan *OR*
    3045 Tan (for
    pillow)
◆ 918 Brick Red
⬗ 3051 Green
■ 3371 Black Brown

Step 2: Straight Stitch
(2 strands)
3371 Black Brown
(bird's legs, beak)

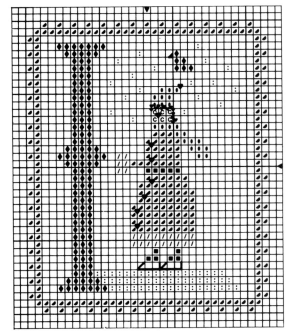

Step 1: Cross-stitch
(2 strands)
◆ 356 Old Red
: 746 Off White
C 754 Peach
◆ 918 Brick Red
/ 3047 Pale Tan
⬗ 3051 Green
■ 3371 Black Brown

Step 2: Backstitch
(2 strands)
3371 Black Brown
(blades)

317 Gray (outline
snowflakes and ice, for
pillow)

Step 3: Straight Stitch
(2 strands)
3371 Black Brown (beak)

Step 4: French Knots
(2 strands)
898 Dk. Brown (eye, hair)
3047 Pale Tan (pom-pom)
3371 Black Brown
(buttons)

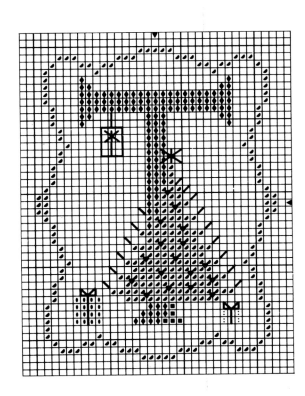

Step 1: Cross-stitch
(2 strands)
◆ 356 Old Red
: 746 Off White *OR*
    356 Old Red (for
    pillow)
◆ 918 Brick Red
⬗ 3051 Green
■ 3371 Black Brown

Step 2: Backstitch
(2 strands)
746 Off White (ribbon on
left gift) *OR*
    3051 Green (for pillow)
918 Brick Red (ribbon on
right gift, candle)
3371 Black Brown
(lantern)

Step 3: Straight Stitch
(2 strands)
746 Off White (tree star) *OR*
    3046 Lt. Tan (for pillow)
3046 Lt. Tan (candle flame)
3051 Green (branch tips) *OR*
    3046 Lt. Tan (for pillow)

Step 4: French Knots
(2 strands)
3046 Lt. Tan (ornaments)

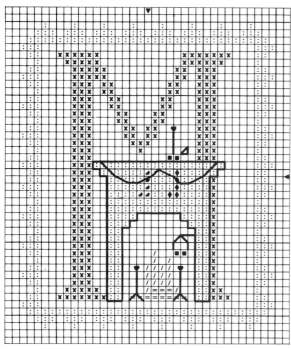

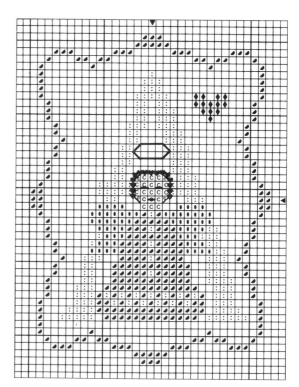

Step 1: Cross-stitch
(2 strands)

=	317 Gray
:	746 Off White
×	869 Dk. Tan
◆	918 Brick Red
/	3046 Lt. Tan
◢	3051 Green
■	3371 Black Brown

Step 2: Backstitch
(2 strands)
317 Gray (mantel)

918 Brick Red (candle)
3051 Green (garland)
3371 Black Brown (candle
holder and pot handles,
pot hanger, andirons)

Step 3: French Knots
(2 strands)
3046 Lt. Tan (candle
flame)
3371 Black Brown
(andiron tops)

Step 1: Cross-stitch
(2 strands)

◆	356 Old Red
:	746 Off White *OR* 918 Brick Red (for pillow)
C	758 Terra Cotta
◆	918 Brick Red
◢	3051 Green

Step 2: Backstitch
(2 strands)
3051 Green (halo)

Step 3: Straight Stitch
(2 strands)
869 Dk. Tan (eyes, mouth)

Step 4: French Knots
(2 strands)
869 Dk. Tan (hair)

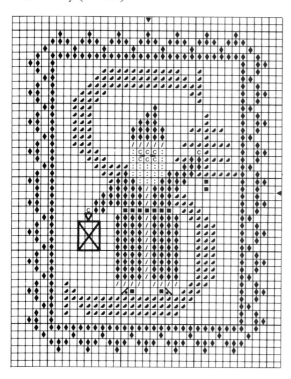

Step 1: Cross-stitch
(2 strands)

:	746 Off White
C	758 Terra Cotta
◆	918 Brick Red
/	3047 Pale Tan
◢	3051 Green
■	3371 Black Brown

Step 2: Backstitch
(2 strands)
3371 Black Brown
(lantern)
317 Gray (outline Santa's
beard for pillow, 1 strand)

Step 3: Straight Stitch
(2 strands)
3371 Black Brown (eyes,
lantern cross bars)

**Dated Diamond
Color Key**

Step 1: Cross-stitch
(2 strands)

×	3045 Tan
◆	918 Brick Red

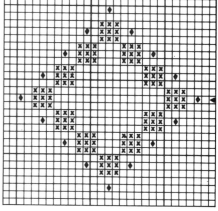

**Numbers for
Date: Color Key**

Step 1: Backstitch
(2 strands)
918 Brick Red

Patriotic Tree Skirt

Instructions are on page 65.
Patterns are full-size.

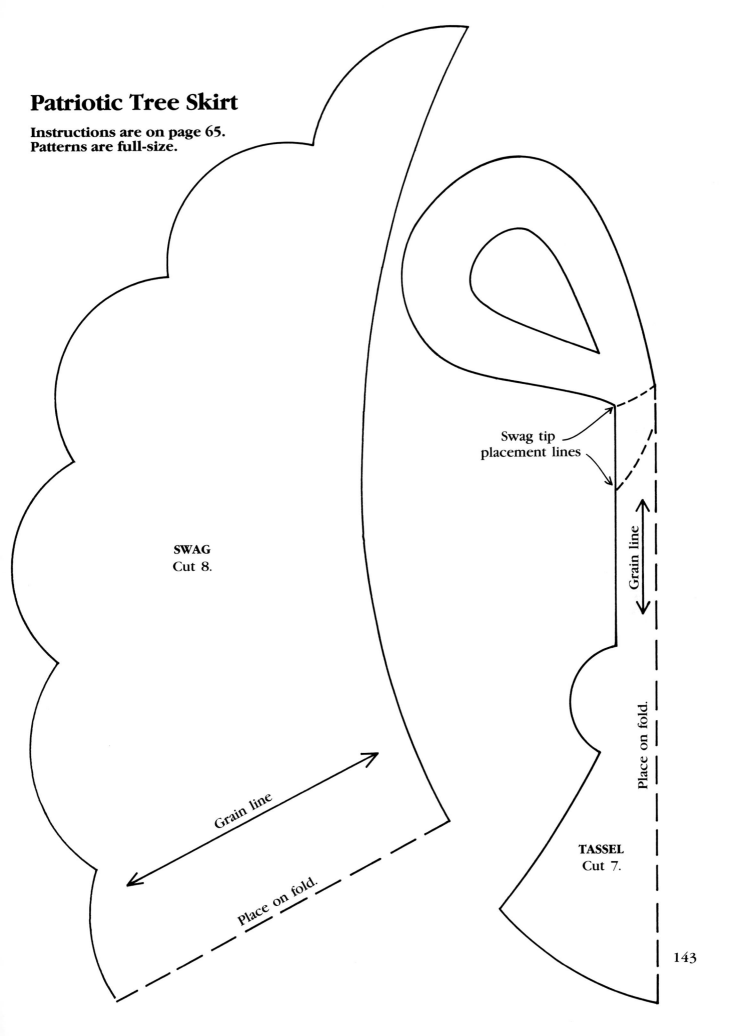

SWAG
Cut 8.

Grain line

Place on fold.

Swag tip placement lines

Grain line

Place on fold.

TASSEL
Cut 7.

143

Stuffed Horse Ornament

Instructions are on page 61.
Pattern is full-size.

M

M

Leave open.

T

BODY
Cut 2 from striped fabric.

Grain line

Front

Seam line

GUSSET
Cut 2 from
striped fabric.

Seam line

BLANKET
Cut 1 from
wool fabric.

Grain
line

144

Front

Cotton Batting Girl and Santa

Instructions are on page 72.
Pattern is
full-size.

Glue
scrap picture
here.

**GIRL
and SANTA**

Paint to
this line.

Paper Hat Ornament

Instructions are on page 61.
Pattern is full-size.

Place on fold.

FEATHER

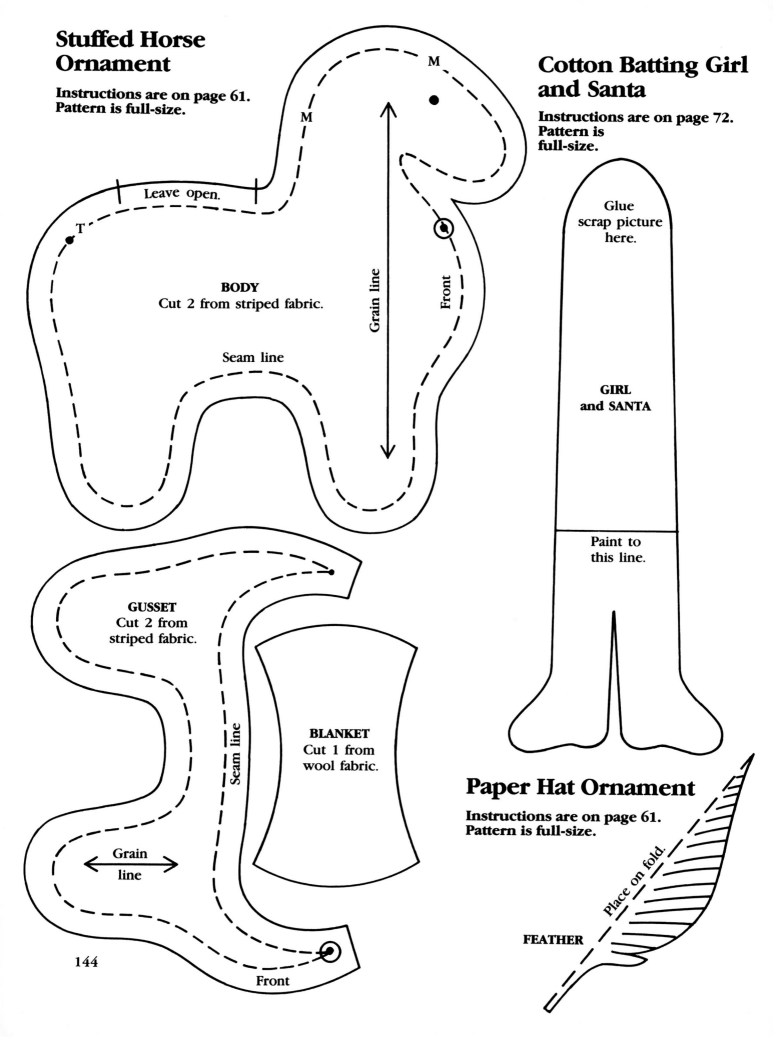

Cross-Stitched Flags

Instructions are on page 62.

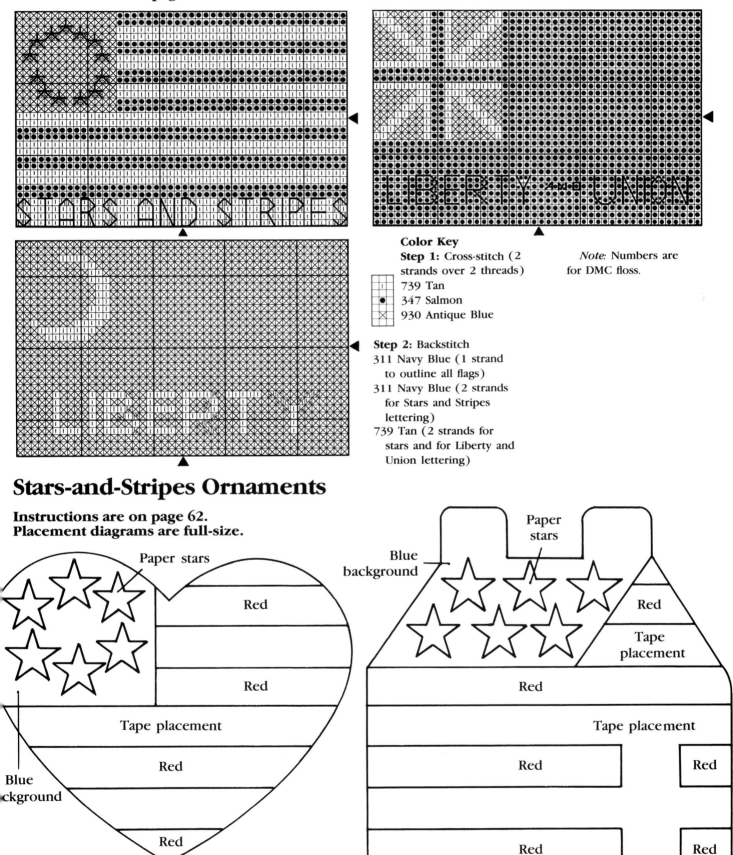

Color Key

Step 1: Cross-stitch (2 strands over 2 threads)

739 Tan
347 Salmon
930 Antique Blue

Note: Numbers are for DMC floss.

Step 2: Backstitch
311 Navy Blue (1 strand to outline all flags)
311 Navy Blue (2 strands for Stars and Stripes lettering)
739 Tan (2 strands for stars and for Liberty and Union lettering)

Stars-and-Stripes Ornaments

Instructions are on page 62.
Placement diagrams are full-size.

Paper stars

Red

Red

Tape placement

Red

Blue background

Red

Blue background

Paper stars

Red

Tape placement

Red

Tape placement

Red

Red

Red

Red

Pink Paper Doll

**Instructions are on page 70.
Pattern is full-size.**

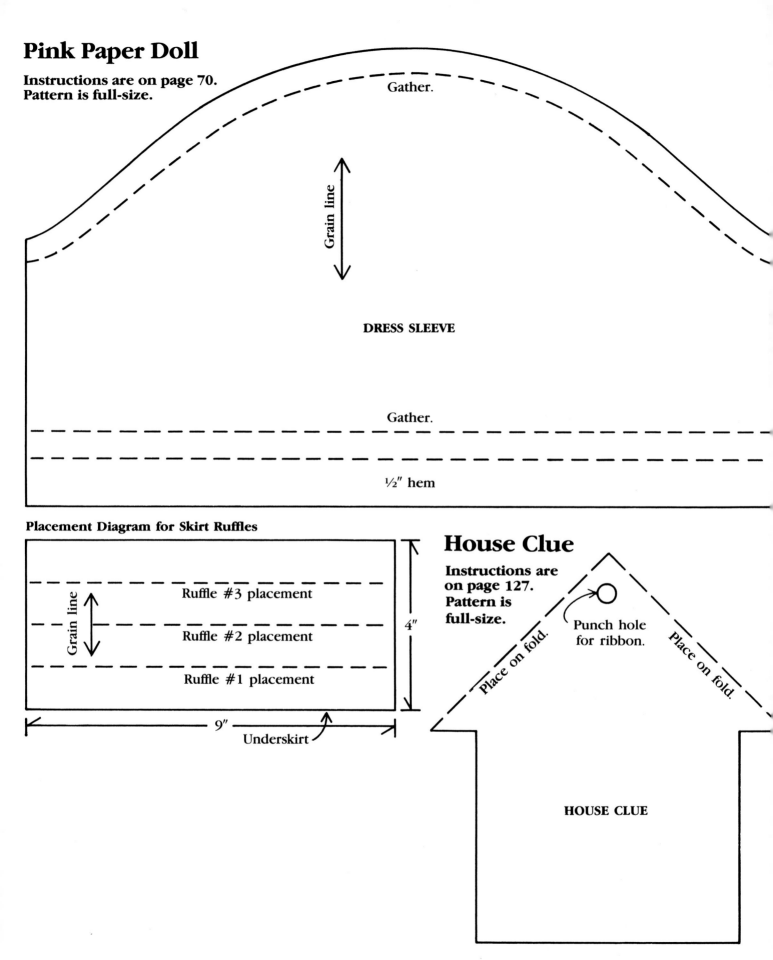

Gather.

Grain line

DRESS SLEEVE

Gather.

½″ hem

Placement Diagram for Skirt Ruffles

Grain line

Ruffle #3 placement

Ruffle #2 placement

Ruffle #1 placement

4″

9″

Underskirt

House Clue

**Instructions are
on page 127.
Pattern is
full-size.**

Place on fold.

Punch hole
for ribbon.

Place on fold.

HOUSE CLUE

Prairie Garlands

Instructions are on page 47.
Pattern is full-size.

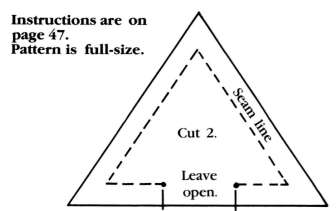

Seam line

Cut 2.

Leave open.

Checkered Santa

Instructions are on page 44.
Pattern is full-size.

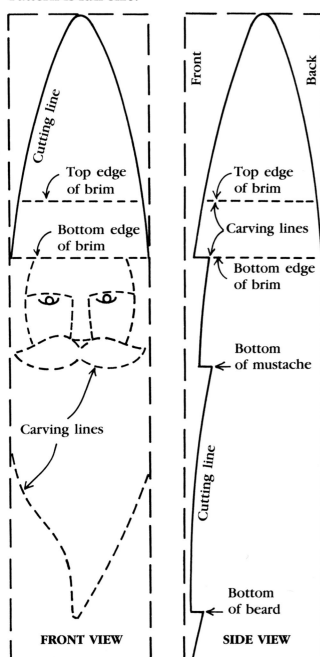

Cutting line

Top edge of brim

Bottom edge of brim

Carving lines

FRONT VIEW

Front

Back

Top edge of brim

Carving lines

Bottom edge of brim

Bottom of mustache

Cutting line

Bottom of beard

SIDE VIEW

Treetop Santa

Instructions are on page 64.

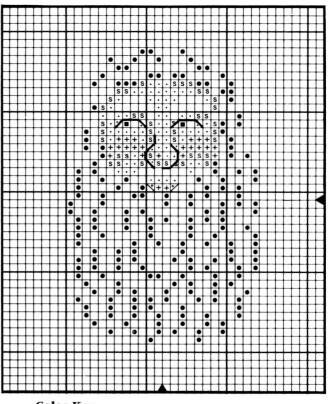

Color Key

Step 1: Cross-Stitch (2 strands)

●	3024 Brown Gray
·	754 Peach
s	758 Terra Cotta
+	352 Coral
■	646 Beaver Gray

Step 2: Backstitch (1 strand)
646 Beaver Gray

Note: Numbers are for DMC floss.

Grapevine Heart Basket

Instructions are on page 90.
Pattern is full-size.

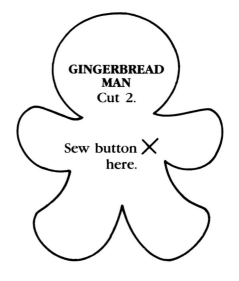

GINGERBREAD MAN
Cut 2.

Sew button ✕ here.

147

Welcome Wall Hanging

Instructions are on page 14.

Center

Center

Match dots and continue chart across page.

148

Cross-stitch on off-white Aida 14. The finished design is 5½" x 9½". The fabric was cut 8½" x 12½".

Color Key: (Use 3 strands over 1 thread.)

815 Garnet
895 Christmas Green
612 Drab Brown
310 Black

Note: Numbers are for DMC floss.

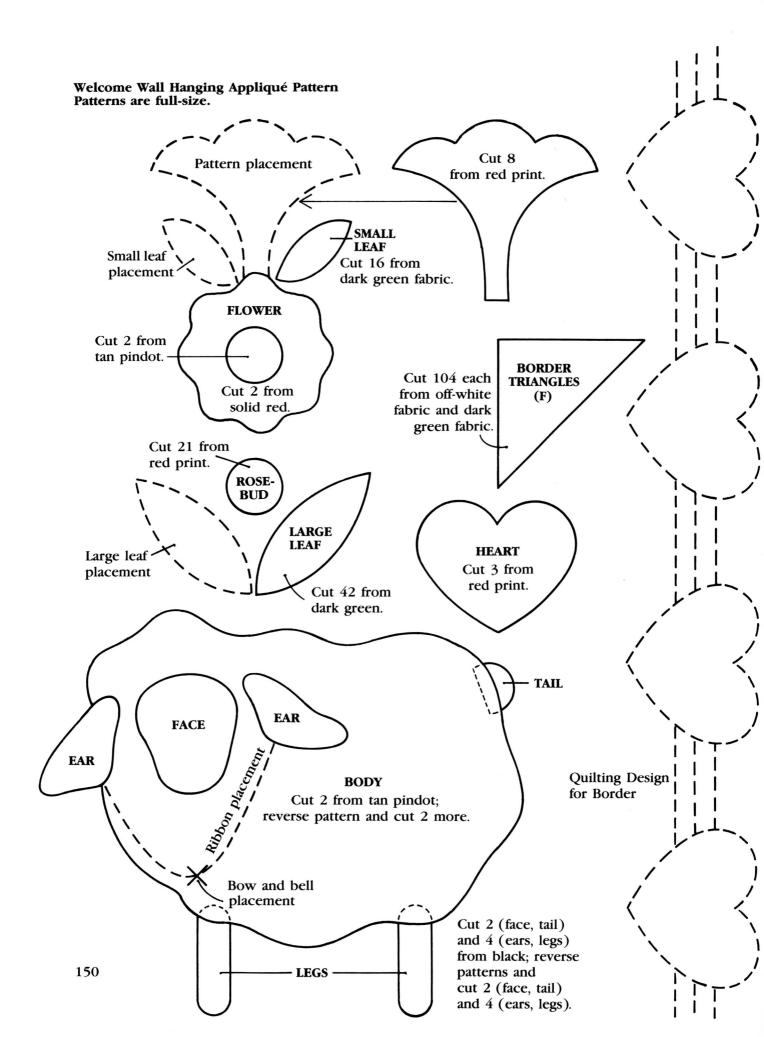

Welcome Wall Hanging Appliqué Pattern
Patterns are full-size.

Pattern placement

Cut 8
from red print.

Small leaf
placement

SMALL LEAF
Cut 16 from
dark green fabric.

FLOWER

Cut 2 from
tan pindot.

Cut 2 from
solid red.

Cut 21 from
red print.

ROSE-BUD

BORDER TRIANGLES (F)

Cut 104 each
from off-white
fabric and dark
green fabric.

LARGE LEAF

Large leaf
placement

Cut 42 from
dark green.

HEART
Cut 3 from
red print.

TAIL

FACE

EAR

EAR

Ribbon placement

BODY
Cut 2 from tan pindot;
reverse pattern and cut 2 more.

Bow and bell
placement

Quilting Design
for Border

Cut 2 (face, tail)
and 4 (ears, legs)
from black; reverse
patterns and
cut 2 (face, tail)
and 4 (ears, legs).

LEGS

150

Welcome Wall Hanging Placement Diagram

Canning Jar Recipe Holder

Instructions are on page 96.
Pattern is full-size.

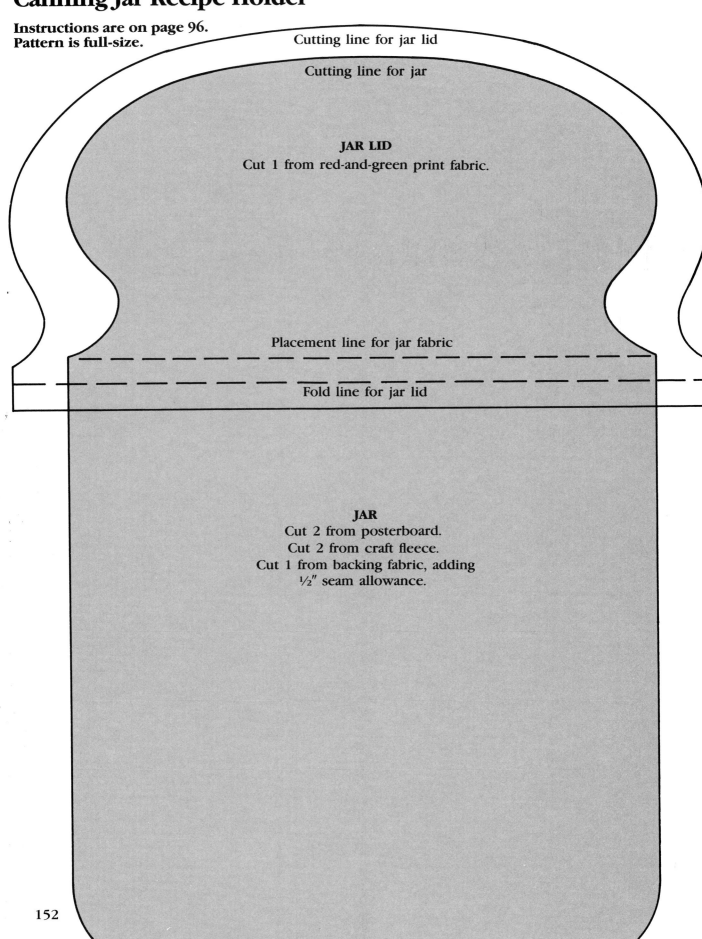

Cutting line for jar lid

Cutting line for jar

JAR LID
Cut 1 from red-and-green print fabric.

Placement line for jar fabric

Fold line for jar lid

JAR
Cut 2 from posterboard.
Cut 2 from craft fleece.
Cut 1 from backing fabric, adding
½″ seam allowance.

Quillwork Ornaments

Instructions are on page 76.
Patterns are full-size.

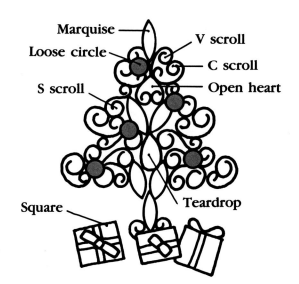

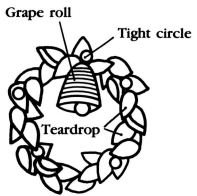

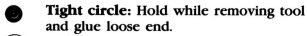

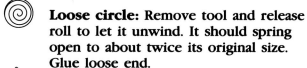

Tight circle: Hold while removing tool and glue loose end.

Loose circle: Remove tool and release roll to let it unwind. It should spring open to about twice its original size. Glue loose end.

Teardrop: Make a loose circle; then pinch one side.

Marquise: Make a loose circle; then pinch opposite sides at the same time.

Square: Pinch into a marquise; turn and pinch opposite sides.

Open heart: Crease strip at center and roll each end toward inside.

V scroll: Crease strip at center and roll ends towards outside.

C scroll: Roll both ends toward center.

S scroll: Roll 1 end toward center. Turn over and roll other end toward center.

Grape roll: Roll a tight circle. Shape into a conical roll by gently pushing center up so that spirals rise in beehive-like shape. After shaping roll, spread a thin layer of glue inside so that roll will retain its shape.

A Christmas Cardigan

Instructions are on page 34.

Standard Knitting Abbreviations
st(s)—stitch(es)
St st—stockinette stitch (k 1 row, p 1 row)
k—knit
p—purl
sl—slip
inc—increase(s) (d) (ing)
rep—repeat
rem—remaining
tog—together
tbl—through back loops
dec—decrease(s) (d) (ing)
pat—pattern
yo—yarn over
*—repeat instructions following asterisk as indicated

Irish Rose Crochet

Instructions are on page 118.

Standard Crochet Abbreviations
beg—beginning
ch—chain
dc—double crochet
hdc—half double crochet
lp—loop
rep—repeat
rnd(s)—round(s)
sc—single crochet
sk—skip
sl st—slip stitch
sp(s)—space(s)
st(s)—stitch(es)

Contributors

Designers

Nena Massey Caldwell, block-print cards, 55.
Susan Cheatham, pinwheels, 63.
Christine Davis, potholders, 117.
Mary Engelbreit, pillows, 32–33.
Connie Formby, Santa, 126; log cabin, 126; stocking, 127; house clue, 127, wrapping paper, 127.
Melissa Gachet, stitching for flags, 63.
Donna Gallagher, treetop Santa, 64.
Nada Gray, Victorian paper dolls, 70.
Barb Griffin, grapevine basket, 88.
Charlotte Hagood, angels, 26; lace stars, 27; horse ornaments, 63; patriotic tree skirt, 66; fruit basket ornaments, 102.
Linda Hendrickson, Bo Peep and sheep, 50.
Homespun Elegance Ltd., cross-stitch pillow and ornaments, 42–43.
Malinda Johnston, quillwork ornaments, 76.
Morgyn Geoffry Owens-Celli, wheat wreath, 19.
Sharon Pierce, checkered Santa, 44.
Maggie Righetti, knitted sweater, 34.

Cecilia C. Robinson, bell ornaments, 58.
St. Nicole Designs, prairie garlands, 47.
Sara Schmitz, cotton batting figures, 72.
Katie Stoddard, mantel swags, 10–11; tin stars, 27.
Mary Lou Taintor, recipe holder, 96.
Carol M. Tipton, construction of painted pillows, 32–33; dancing children pillow, 36; tree skirt, 37; construction of fruit basket ornaments, 102.
Becky Tuttle, roly-poly Santa, 45.
The Vanessa-Ann Collection, cross-stitch flags, 63.
Joan Vibert, house and heart ornaments, 63.
Suzanne Wall, wall hanging, 14.
Julie A. Wilson, embossed cards, 55.
Judy A. Zbyrowski, coverlet ornament and stocking, 48–49.

Photographers

Gary Clark, 21.
Colleen Duffley, left 10, 11–14, 18, 28–31, 45, lower left and right 56, 57, 67, 76, 96, 101–102, background 120–121.
Mary-Gray Hunter, 60, 63–64, 66.

Beth Maynor, 4–9.
Art Meripol, 49.
John O'Hagan, senior photographer, cover, 2–3, right 10, 16–17, 19, 22–27, 32–34, 36, 39–41, 47, 50, 55, upper right 56, 58–59, 68–70, 72–75, 78–81, 83, 85, 88, 92, 95, 98, 103–105, 109–114, 117–118, insets 120–121, 122–123, 126–127.
Melissa Springer, 37, 42–44.

Photostylists

Kay Clarke, 101.
Connie Formby, 126–127.
Susan Merrill, 83, 85, 88, 92, 95, 98, 103–105, 109–111, 114, 117–118, 122–123.
Glenda Parker, center 22, top left 23.
Katie Stoddard, 10–11, 19, upper left and right 22, bottom and right 23, 27, 32–34, 37, 42–44, top 56, 60, 63–64, 66, 78–79.

Sources

• Page 21—wheat-weaving supplies catalog: legal-size SASE to Doxie Keller Enterprises, 127 W. 30th Ave., Hutchinson, KS 67502

• Page 30—designs: The Mary Engelbreit Co., 12 N. Gore, St. Louis, MO 63119
• Page 46—crepe-wool hair: All Cooped Up, 560 South State St., B1, Orem, UT 84058
• Pages 48–49, 105—chalkware catalog: $4 to Vaillancourt Folk Art, 145 Armsby Rd., Sutton, MA 01590
• Page 57—stamping supplies catalog: $3 to Personal Stamp Exchange, 345 McDowell Blvd., Suite 324, Petaluma, CA 94954
• Page 60—eagle, sunburst; page 71—paper dolls; page 72—scrap pictures (catalog): $2.25 to Gerlachs of Lecha, P.O. Box 213, Emmaus, PA 18049
• Page 71—book: $14.50 to Pennsylvania State University Press, Barbara Bldg., Suite C, 820 N. University Dr., University Park, PA 16802
• Page 76—quilling supplies catalog: $1.50 to Lake City Craft Co., Rte. 1, Box 637, Highlandville, MO 65669
• Page 94—herb catalog: Fox Hill Farm, 444 W. Michigan Ave., Box 9, Parma, MI 49269

Acknowledgments

Special thanks to:
Margaret Allen Northen
Susan Ramey Wright

Index

General

Appliqué
  paper-patch method, 15
  wall hanging, 14–15

Cards
  block-print, 54
  embossed, 54–55
  framing collections, 18
  stamped greeting, 56
Crochet potholders, 112–113, 118–119
Cross-stitch
  decorating with, 17, 39–41
  ornaments and pillow, 42–43
  ornaments, coverlet, 48–49
  ornaments, cross-stitched flags, 58–59, 62
  stocking, coverlet, 49
  wall hanging, 14–15

Decorating
  old-fashioned farmhouse, 4–9
  swags, taffeta mantel, 10–11
  with candles, 22–23
  with Christmas cards, 18
  with crafts, 16–17
  with cross-stitch, 17, 39–41
  with paper dolls, 70–71
  with potpourri, 78–79

Dolls
  Bo Peep and sheep, 50–53
  girl, cotton batting, 72
  pink paper, 70–71
  Santa, cotton batting, 72
  Santa, roly-poly, 46

Embroidery
  pillow cover, 37
  pillow, Santa, 32–33
  pillow, snowman, 32–33
  tree skirt, 38

Garlands
  braided, prairie, 47
  chunky, prairie, 47
  cross-stitch, 42
  foil paper, diamond, 80–81, 86
  foil paper, pleated, 80–81, 86
  prairie point, 2–3, 47
Gift wrapping and packaging
  basket, grapevine heart, 90
  boxes for foods, 80–83
  buttons, plaid-covered, 11
  for children, gift mystery search, 127
  for children, stocking stuffers, 127
  jar toppers, 80–83
  log box with candy, 126
  nuts, gilded, 80–81, 86
  paper, photocopying color designs, 80–81, 82, 127

Santa-in-the-Box, 126
  stamping, 56–57
  stars, lace, 25, 27
  with photographs, 127
  with quillwork, 76

Knitting
  cardigan, 34–35

Napkins, stamped, 56

Ornaments
  angels, 24–26
  basket, wooden fruit, 102
  coverlet, cross-stitched, 48–49
  cross-stitched, 42
  flags, cross-stitched, 58–59, 62
  girl, cotton batting, 72
  hat, paper, 61
  horse, stuffed, 61
  jingle bell, 58–59, 62
  lace stars, 25, 27
  paper doll, pink, 70–71
  pinwheels, fabric, 59–60
  quillwork, tree, 77
  quillwork, wreath, 77
  Santa, cotton batting, 72
  Santa, treetop, 64–65
  stars-and-stripes, 62
  tin stars, 25, 27
  wheat, courtier's knot, 2–3, 19-21

Package toppers
  buttons, plaid-covered, 11

jar toppers, 80–83
  nuts, gilded, 80–81, 86
  stamping, 56–57
  stars, lace, 25, 27
  with quillwork, 76
Pillows
  cover, dancing children, 37
  cross-stitched, 42–43
  Santa, 32–33
  snowman, 32–33
Potholders
  hexagon, crocheted, 113, 118–119
  square, crocheted, 112, 119
Potpourri
  apple-evergreen, 78–79
  citrus-evergreen, 78
  drying hint, 79
  rose petal, 79

Quillwork, 76–77
Quilting
  wall hanging, 14–15

Santas
  checkered, 44–45
  cotton batting, 72
  in-a-box, 126
  pillow, 32–33
  roly-poly, 46
  treetop, 64
Stamping, 54–57
  cards, block-print, 54
  cards, greeting, 56
  napkins, 56
  pad, making, 56
  sampler, 57
  with fruit, 56
Stockings
  coverlet, 49
  stuffers, 127

Stuffed animals
    horse ornament, 61
    sheep, Bo Peep and,
        50–53
Swags
    plaid taffeta, 11
    red and green taffeta,
        10–11
Sweaters
    Christmas cardigan,
        34–35

Tea-dyeing, 64
Towels, stamped, 56
Tree
    cutting, 120–121
    patriotic, 60–66
    skirt, dancing
        children, 38
    skirt, patriotic, 65–66
    treetop Santa, 64–65
    wheat ornament, 2–3,
        19–21

Wall hanging, 14–15
Wheat
    bellpull, Christmas
        wreath, 19
    courtier's knot
        ornament, 2–3, 19–21
    wreath, 2, 19–21
Wood crafts
    ornaments,
        stars-and-stripes, 62
    Santa, checkered, 44–45
Wreaths
    apple fan, 9
    bellpull, 19
    bittersweet, 16–17
    quillwork, 77
    wheat, courtier's knot,
        2, 19–21

Recipes

Appetizers
    Almond-Chicken
        Stuffed Pastry, 111
    Avocado Beef Rolls,
        111
    Brick and Blue
        Potatoes, 100
    Cheddar Cheesecake,
        98
    Cheese Bites and
        Olives, 100
    Cheese in a Blanket,
        100
    Chicken Pâté,
        116–117
    Chili Rellenos, 97
    Gruyère and Spinach
        Tart, 117
    Pesto and Cheese
        Terrine, 100–101
    Pesto Spread, 111
    Pineapple-Cheese
        Welcome Spread,
        101
    Salsa, Black-Eyed Pea,
        124
    Zucchini with Asiago
        and Cheddar, 97

Beverages
    Candy Cane, Hot 122
    Coffee, Coconut
        Cream, 122–123
    Cranberry Cordial,
        118
    Ice Ring, 118
    Milk Chocolate
        Cream, 122
    Tea, Hot Orange
        Cream, 116
    Tea Punch, Chilled
        Apple, 118
Breads and rolls
    Bagel Bread, 97
    Cornbread, Bacon and
        Green Chili, 124
    Nut Cracker Bread,
        Toasted, 123
    Orange Rum Rolls,
        90–91
    Popovers, Bacon, 125
    Scones, English Tea,
        115

Butter
    Brandied Butter,
        Whipped, 115
    Chambord Butter,
        Whipped, 115
    Ginger-Lime Butter,
        115

Cakes
    Cheesecake with
        cookies and
        strawberries, 110
    Chocolate Cake,
        Golden White-,
        108–109
    Fudge Fruitcake,
        Princess, 106
    Lemon Puffed
        Pancake, 93
    Lemony Almond Cake,
        89
    Lime Torte, Angel, 91
    Soufflé, Café au Lait,
        106–107
Candies
    Caramel Christmas
        Trees, 106
    Caramel Fans, Lace,
        107
    Maple Syrup Candies,
        94
    Orange Rind, Candied,
        89
Chocolate
    Brownies, 86
    Choclava, 84
    Cinnamon-Almond
        Mocha Mix, 84
    Coconut Gems, 87
    Liqueur, 84
    Peanutty Chocolate
        Apples, 87
    Praline Truffles, 82
    Sauce, Hot Fudge, 82
    Toffee Trail Mix, 87
Cookies
    Lemon Bars, 91
    Orange Florentines,
        89
    Shortbread coated
        with chocolate, 110

Strawberry Sandwich
        Cookies, 116

Frostings, glazes, and
    toppings
    Buttercream Frosting,
        Spiced, 106
    Chocolate Frosting,
        White-, 108–109
    Lemon Curd, 93
    Orange Cream, 93
    Orange Rum Glaze, 91

Gift foods
    cheesecloth bags with
        herbs, 111
    chocolate, 82–87
    pepper mill, filled, 111
    Rice Pilaf Mix, 111
    sugars and syrups, 94–95

Pies and pastries
    Citrus Tarts, Tiny, 93
    Croquembouche,
        Shimmering, 107
    Orange Chess Pie,
        Country, 91
    Puffs, Cream, 107

Salads
    Broccoli Salad, 125
    Coleslaw, Green and
        Red Pepper, 124
Sandwiches,
    Turkey, 116
Stew, Andouille Sausage,
    125
Sugars and syrups
    Lemon Verbena Sugar,
        Layered, 94
    Mint-Flavored Sugar
        Cubes, 94
    Pansies, Crystallized, 94
    Rose Geranium Sugar,
        94
    Rose Petal Syrup, 94–95
    Spun Sugar Halo, 109
    Spun Sugar Nests, 108